6-1-70

The *Amistad* Affair

The *Amistad* Affair
by
Christopher Martin, pseud.

Edwin Palmer Hoyt

Abelard-Schuman
London   New York   Toronto

LONDON	NEW YORK	TORONTO
Abelard-Schuman	Abelard-Schuman	Abelard-Schuman
Limited	Limited	Canada Limited
8 King St. WC2	257 Park Ave. So.	200 Yorkland Blvd.

An Intext Publisher

Printed in the United States of America

Contents

1540721

1/The African Slave Trade

Slavery and slave trade had been an acceptable way of life in western Europe during the eighteenth century, but by the beginning of the next century men of conscience were rebelling against this cruelty. By the summer of 1839 nearly all nations of the civilized West were agreed, at least in theory, that the trade in human beings must be brought to an end.

In 1802 Denmark became the first European power to abolish the trade. England followed. The United States, which had in 1794 recognized the immorality of the trade by prohibiting American citizens to participate in slave trade with foreign countries, forbade importation of slaves into the United States in 1808. In 1815 Portugal — one of the leading nations in the trade — also forbade commerce in human bodies above the equator and moved to stop the trade entirely by 1830. Under Napoleon France had abandoned the slave trade, and the emperor's edict was confirmed by successive governments. The Netherlands and Sweden stopped trading in human lives. By 1835 even Spain agreed to put an end to slave trading. In this age of Christian enlightenment it was finally realized everywhere that all men were creatures with souls.

The most severe blow against the slave trade was inaugurated by England, which proposed to the nations that mixed commissions be established at places where trade was most active. One such place was Sierra Leone, the central point of departure for the slave trade from Africa. Another was Havana, which was a central point of arrival for slave traders, who then moved their human cargoes into the Caribbean islands and the southern United States.[1]

But how effective could abolition of this lucrative trade be when a huge segment of the Western world's economy depended on the constant replenishment of a cheap source of human labor? It is true the United States had abolished slave trade early in the nineteenth century, but that meant only external slave trade. The breeding of slaves as cattle and the trading in slaves among the states, was not abolished. In 1820 it was apparent that illegal importation of slaves had not been stopped (approximately 250,000 slaves were imported into the United States between 1808 and 1860). Congress declared importing slaves to be "piracy" and punishable by hanging.[2] But it persisted.

In the 1830's the Spanish and the Portuguese, allied with Americans, were the most consistent violators of international conventions against slave trading. The mixed commissions had the power to fine and punish offenders; most important, they had the right to free the slaves, send them back to Africa, and break up and sell the ships and possessions of the slavers. Punishment was meted out scores of times, and yet, so great were the rewards of slaving that the trade scarcely diminished.

From January 1, 1829, to January 1, 1836, twenty-nine Spanish slave vessels, carrying 8,312 slaves, were condemned by the mixed court at Havana. In the six months between June 30, 1838, and the end of the year, eleven Spanish ships were condemned at Sierra Leone simply because they were fitted out for the slave trade.[3] Yet for every vessel captured and broken up, another was supplied. Far too many of these ships, usually low, fast schooners, were supplied by the God-fearing shipbuilders of New England, who would have rolled their eyes piously at heaven had they been accused of perpetuating the slave trade.

Sentiment in the United States for . and against slavery began to harden. The first petition for emancipation of all slaves was presented to Congress in 1790 by The Society of Friends, but the situation reached a critical stage only with the first session of the 35th Congress, which opened in December, 1835. During 1836, Congress was flooded with petitions and memorials urging federal intervention to abolish slavery in all the states. The argument that eventually led to American disunion had begun.[4]

Two years later the Spanish Crown issued a royal order to the captain general of the island of Cuba, directing him to stamp out slave trade there, and on June 20, 1838, it was decreed that only a legitimate slave proprietor could transfer his slaves from one port in Cuba to another by sea. No more slaves could be brought into Cuba for transport anywhere else. In Spanish terms, there were two kinds of slaves — *bozals* and *ladinos*. A *bozal* was a slave imported from Africa for the use of a Spanish slave-owner in the conduct of his own affairs. This slave was not to be traded anywhere or shipped by sea. A *ladino* was a second-generation slave. He could be shipped and sold within the Spanish possessions, but only if his owner possessed proper documents showing that he had been imported into Spanish territory before the Crown's new regulations had been put into effect.

But in the effulgent atmosphere of rotting Spain, governors and lesser officials were prone to overlook such niceties as the content of the law in favor of the form — for a fee. It was never difficult for a slave trader to purchase the necessary papers permitting slaves imported from Africa into Cuba to be trans-shipped to the United States.[5]

By the summer of 1839 opinions on slave trade and slavery drew obvious lines in the United States between North and

South. Throughout New England anti-slavery organizations were being formed and encouraged openly. They were flooding the entire country with literature about slavery. In the South, business organizations were strengthening their position to preserve slavery at all costs. And even though it could be proved that slavery was economically unsound for agriculture, that argument was being submerged under the emotional arguments. As long as the Southerners believed that the people of New England were trying to destroy their livelihood and turn the South into a colony of the North, no intellectual arguments had much effect. Southern planters, merchants, and shipowners winked at the federal laws and combined to bring in slaves by the thousands.

Newspapers lined up on one side or the other. Political parties did, too, with the Whigs growing strong on anti-slavery arguments (although this was the heyday of Henry Clay, a slaveholder) and the Democrats making the compromise that was to destroy their party in 1860.

Very influential among the anti-slavery newspapers was the Hartford *Courant,* which had combined with the Connecticut *Courant* and was the most important newspaper in the state. It was also pro-Whig or pulled no punches in either cause. Its favorite whipping boys were the Democratic President Martin van Buren, a Democratic newspaper, the Hartford *Times,* and slavery in any of its manifestations. The editors assiduously searched their exchange copies of the newspapers of the nation — and of the world — for ammunition that would help them slay their enemies and raise the flags of their friends.

In 1839 the *Courant* remarked on an event that occurred in June, which revealed the status of slave trade in Caribbean waters. Her Majesty's sloop *Snake* arrived in these waters with the mission of destroying the slave trade and in conjunction with the *Pickle,* a British schooner, proceeded to do so. Soon the *Snake* captured the *Coridad Cuba,* a Spanish slaver,

which it encountered off the coast of Puerto Rico. Boarding
the suspicious ship, the officers discovered 171 slaves aboard.

The *Pickle* had a slightly different experience. Off the Cuban
coast, on June 14, the captain saw a suspicious vessel standing
for the Isle of Pines and decided to investigate. His suspicion
was aroused because the vessel was a schooner, sleek and low
and fast, and was obviously trying to avoid him. He ran up a
signal, ordering the schooner to stop. The schooner rushed on
toward the safety of Cuban waters. The *Pickle* fired a shot
across her bows. The schooner did not even hesitate. The
Pickle fired several more shots, still not trying to hit the ship.
The schooner bore on.

Through his glass the captain of the *Pickle* could see seamen
on the schooner piling on the canvas and throwing casks and
other objects overboard. There could be no further question:
the schooner was desperately trying to escape, and since there
was no reason for that except piracy, smuggling, or slavery, the
Pickle would be within its rights to blast the schooner out of
the water — if it could catch up.

The chase was long and hard, as the slaver was nearly as
fast as the *Pickle*. The captain ordered his gunnery officer
to load with grape and canister shot. These would be effective
against personnel, but would not be likely to penetrate the
decks and kill the innocent blacks — if indeed the ship was
a slaver.

Six hours the chase lasted, the *Pickle* gaining very slowly on
the mystery ship, whose crewmen threw themselves flat on the
deck with every gun report, and then leaped up into action
once the shots had passed. At last the schooner hoisted Portuguese colors. This, of course, revealed nothing about its mission,
but it did mean that if by some chance it was an innocent
vessel, the captain of the *Pickle* would be in for some rough
moments with his admiral.

But the schooner gave no indication of innocence. At night,
under cover of darkness, it slid into shore and stood two cable

lengths off land, just outside shoal water. But from the deck, the British captain could see, despite the darkness, what was happening aboard the other vessel. They were throwing Negroes into the sea. He had been right; it was a slaver. He sent off boats, filled with men armed with muskets, pistols, and cutlasses.

The crew of the slaver, seeing that they would be boarded within a few minutes, threw themselves over the side, to swim ashore and seek safety from a British court. Their escape was successful, if their voyage was not.

On boarding the slaver the British sailors discovered that it was the *Sierra del Pilar,* seventy-eight days out of Africa, carrying 180 Negroes. At least they found 180 Negroes. Talking with those few who understood a few fragments of European languages, they learned that the original slave cargo had consisted of 225 Negroes, but several had died on the journey and others had been thrown overboard in a desperate attempt to hide the evidence.

That night the British put a prize crew aboard the *Sierra del Pilar* and took it to Havana, where it would be handed over to the mixed commission. The Negroes were lucky, for they would be manumitted — set free and returned to Africa to make their way back to their homes. The *Sierra del Pilar* would be sold for its parts and would never again sail in Western waters — at least not under that name.

Reporting all this, the editors of the Hartford *Courant* commented that the story, was one which "no man who possesses the common feelings of humanity can read without a thrill of indignation and horror." And they added: "Yet scenes of a similar character are enacted almost daily — yes, in this nineteenth century — among Christians — who boast of the progress of philanthropy and religion! — This country should rebuke by *actions* as well as words such inhuman conduct, and make an energetic effort to put a stop to the horrible traffic in slaves."[6]

Slavery itself was evil. Slave trade was evil. But most evil of all, in the eyes of non-slaveholding civilized men, were the conditions under which slavery was practiced. "The scene of misery and filth that presented itself on board [the *Sierra del Pilar*] is inconceivable."[7]

To white gentlefolk, living far from the regions of slavery, such maltreatment of human beings was indeed inconceivable; but to thousands of other people in the world, slavery was strictly a business, one in which an unscrupulous trader could hope to grow rich very quickly, with luck.

A typical account of a slave voyage was given by Brantz Mayer in *Twenty Years of an African Slaver*. Because this book was written in 1854 as a popular and sensational study of slave trading makes it suspect as a propaganda document, but the essential facts about slave trade in Africa and across the seas remains very close to facts revealed by other sources. The book is supposedly based on the journals and memoranda of Captain Canot, who spent a score of years in West African slave trade. The accounting for one voyage indicates the reason men braved the gauntlet of naval vessels in 1827 to run between the West African coast and Cuba:[8]

Expenses Out

Cost of *La Fortuna*, a 90-ton schooner	$ 3,700.00
Fitting out, sails, carpenter and cooper's bills	2,500.00
Provisions for crew and slaves	1,115.00
Wages advanced to 18 men before the mast	900.00
Wages advanced to captain, mates, boatswain, cook and steward	440.00
200,000 cigars and 500 doubloons, cargo	10,900.00
Clearance and hush money	200.00
	19,755.00
Commission at 5 percent	987.00
Full cost of voyage out	$20,742.00

Expenses Home

Captain's head money at $8 a head	$ 1,746.00
Mate's head money at $4 a head	873.00
Second mate's and boatswain's head money at $2 each	873.00
Captain's wages	219.78
First mate's wages	175.56
Second mate's and boatswain's wages	307.12
Cook and steward's wages	264.00
Eighteen sailors' wages	1,972.00
	$27,172.46

Expenses in Havana

Government officers at $8 per head	$ 1,736.00
My commission on 217 slaves, Expenses off	5,565.00
Consignees' commissions	3,873.00
217 slave dresses at $2 each	634.00
Extra expenses of all kinds	1,000.00
Total expense	$39,980.46

Returns

Value of vessel at auction	$3,950.00
Proceeds of 217 slaves	77,469.00
	81,419.00
Expenses	39,980.46
Net profit	$41,438.54

The net profit of more than $41,000 represented the cost of perhaps ten small ships, which meant that a man with so much capital could retire after one successful slave voyage and go into an honest business. Half a dozen such voyages would, in the late 1820's, make him a very wealthy man. A decade later the value of slaves rose by 50 percent because of the embargo against the slave trade, and although the risks were greater, the rewards were so great that conscienceless men of many nations were willing to take the chance and work the slave trade. The profits had increased greatly since the middle of the eighteenth century, when slave trading was legal. Then, according to slave trader Nicholas Owen, "a slave is rated at 20 country bars (pounds), which when brought down here we buy for 45 or 50 bars and again sold on board a ship produces 80 ship's bars, which is above 100 country bars or crowns, a considerable profit. . . ."[9]

Naturally, to insure such profits, the captain of a slave trading vessel did his best to keep the cargo whole and sound. This was particularly true if the captain was in business for himself, but in most cases the captains of slavers were merely hired hands who had a share of the proceeds, and their understanding of such matters as simple health safeguards and sanitation left much to be desired.

Under the most favorable conditions, a slave shipment could not be called anything but inhuman. The Negroes were assembled by the trader in the *barracoon*, or slave pen, which was almost always in a city or village near the sea, to allow the fresh coastal winds to blow away the rheums and diseases that afflicted men crammed together in captivity. The *barracoon* was usually a huge hut divided into cubicles. Slaves were jammed into these cubicles. If the slave dealer was handling cargo for several merchants, he would brand his captives with the initials of their owners. The branding was done with small irons in order not to disfigure the slaves and reduce their value.

Africans were assembled in ones and twos and dozens, sometimes enslaved for debt, sometimes captured by enemies and sold, sometimes acquired by dealers through bartering with kings and local nobility.

When a slave ship came into harbor, its captain began negotiating for the number of slaves wanted, or the slave dealer would order his own ships and send them across to Havana. Once the proper number of slaves was assembled in the *barracoon* the sailing day would be set. On the day before sailing the slave dealer would arrange a huge feast for his slaves. It was good business to "feed them up" on the last day, for it made them content and less liable to give trouble when taken aboard ship. Once aboard, they were stripped and sent below into the hold. In a few slave ships the men and women were separated. Sometimes the special slave holds were only 30 or 36 inches from floor to ceiling. If the slaver were a careful man, he would keep the children on deck, under sails and tarpaulins to protect them from the weather.

The slaves were fed twice a day, at ten in the morning and four in the afternoon. First a bucket of salt water was brought into the slave quarters — a bucket for each ten men if the ship captain was generous. The slaves washed in this water. Then the meal, called a *kidd*, was brought on in buckets. Crewmen or slave monitors supervised the feeding. The Negroes were ordered to dip their hands into the mess — it might be rice, farina, yams, or beans — and then they were ordered to eat. The guards reported on the eating habits of the slaves. If they did not eat properly, they were flogged. If they got sick, they were taken out of the slave hold for inspection, and if they were seriously ill, they were thrown overboard.

Most males were kept chained in groups of five or ten during the entire voyage, iron collars around their necks. They were jammed together in rows. If they were crowded too tightly, if the weather grew bad, if they were not taken out for air, they might develop any of a number of diseases. Worst of all these ills was the "bloody flux," a dysentery that killed very quickly in the holds of the slave ships and might spread to captain and crew as well.

So it was good business to bring the slaves out for air frequently, to keep them clean and sloshed down with salt water, to remove the offal from their kennels often. Any slaver could

tell by the manner in which the slaves ate how well they
were bearing the voyage. An intelligent captain spent a little
money on lime juice and vinegar to keep the slaves' mouths
clean and keep them from contracting scurvy; a little money
on tobacco, which they smoked through communal pipes; a
little on fish oil for their bodies to ease the ravages of the chains
and collars.

On a clean slaver the profits were better, so some captains
made sure that their slaves were brought up from the holds
each morning (unless a sail came in sight), that the slave
decks were scrubbed with salt water and disinfectants, and that
the slaves were exercised on deck.

Sometimes the Negroes were left above decks until sundown,
but they were always sent below for the night, into the dank
dimness of the horror chamber. At dusk the second mate and
the boatswain descended into the hold, and the slaves were
forced below. Those on the starboard side were made to lie on
their right sides facing the bow of the ship, for it was believed
that lying on the right side made it easier for the heart to work
properly. Each slave was so cramped that his head lay in the
lap of the slave behind him.

The slaves on the port side were disposed the same way,
except that they faced the stern of the ship, lying on their
right sides. Then, when the cargo was all settled for the night,
the hatches were secured and the mate and boatswain went
on deck, locking the hatches behind them.

Night was the terrible time on the slaver, when men rolled
and stank in their juices, and when the sick died and the well
became sick. In stormy weather the slaves were lucky if they
got one meal in three, and when they received it they were
lucky if they could eat in the stench of vomit and offal.

To preserve order among the slaves when they had to be
kept below during rough weather monitors were chosen and
given cat-o'-nine-tails whips with which they kept the others

from moving about. The monitors were rewarded with an extra ration of food or a tot of rum.

In the tropics, even with ventilators in the sides and decks of the ships, it was sometimes murderous to keep the slaves penned so tightly below, and about half the slaves would be allowed to sleep on deck, under guard.

These were ideal conditions; too often the captains were terrified by the possibility of a slave rebellion, or the weather turned foul, or some of the crew enjoyed mistreating the slaves. Under the best conditions the slave's voyage was only bearable; he was treated like an animal. Under the worst conditions he was lucky to come out alive. It was common talk that sharks followed the slavers across the oceans, feasting on the corpses that were thrown over the side day after day as the Africans died in the heat and filth.

Slave ships came in all sizes, carrying as few as two hundred or three hundred Negroes and as many as eight hundred more. Captain Canot described one voyage that showed what might happen to a ship carrying a cargo of eight hundred slaves, picked up on the east coast of Africa and destined for the Caribbean.

Off the Cape of Good Hope the vessel encountered bad weather. The captain fell ill with fever and became insensible, then raving. The word spread that several slaves were ill with smallpox.

Smallpox!

It was a dreaded word on a slaver, as dreadful as "bloody flux."

"The gale had lasted nine days without intermission," Canot said, "and during all this time with so much violence that it was impossible to take off the gratings, release the slaves, purify the decks, or rig the wind sails. When the first lull occurred, a thorough inspection of the eight hundred was made, and *a death announced.*"

This death was the cause for secret panic among the officers of the ship. The body was swiftly spirited out of the slave hold, examined and seen to be poxed, and then slid over the side. The secret was kept from the crew and Negroes that night.

"When breakfast was over on that fatal morning, I determined to visit the slave deck myself," said Captain Canot, "and ordering an abundant supply of lanterns, descended in the cavern, which still reeked horribly with human vapor, even after ventilation."

The officers counseled. They might use laudanum. Sometimes this strong medicine was used to put slaves out of their misery and protect the living from infection. But in this case the smallpox had spread too far and too fast to make it useful or possible. Nine men were down with the disease. The account goes on:

> Accordingly these wretched beings were at once sent to the forecastle as a hospital and given in charge to the vaccinated or inoculated as nurses. The hold was then ventilated and limed; yet before the gale abated, our sick list was increased to thirty. The hospital could hold no more. Twelve of the sailors took the infection and fifteen corpses had been cast into the sea.
>
> All reserve was now at an end. Body after body fed the deep, and still the gale held on. At last, when the wind and waves had lulled so much as to allow the gratings to be removed from our hatches, our consternation knew no bounds when we found that nearly all the slaves were dead or dying with the distemper. I will not dwell on the scene or our sensations. It is a picture that must gape with all its horrors before the least vivid imagination. Yet there was no time for languor or sentimental sorrow. Twelve of the stoutest survivors were ordered to drag out the dead from among the ill, and though they were constantly drenched with rum to brutalize them, still we were forced to aid the gang with reckless volunteers from our crew, who, arming their hands with tarred mittens, flung the foetid masses of putrefaction into the sea!

In a few days, when the pestilence appeared to be ended, they were able to count the number of surviving slaves aboard the slaver. The crew had been reduced by a dozen, but the cargo — of 800 slaves there were only 497 left alive and they were as thin as skeletons!

Sometimes slaves rebelled. Captain Canot described one voyage he took in the schooner *La Estrella*, which he had purchased in Havana from a firm that had in turn purchased the ship from its American builders. Captain Canot had fitted the ship out as a slaver and gone slaving away from his usual haunts. Consequently, he ended up with a cargo of 450 slaves, but with not one person aboard the slaver who understood the dialect of the captives. There was no way the slaves could tell of the causes for discontent. If they complained, they were thrashed.

When the ship was a few days out from port, bound for Cuba, one slave leaped overboard after he had been freed for a moment on deck. That same night another slave choked himself to death — and the officers of the slaver prepared for trouble. The passage might take anywhere from sixty to ninety days, and this was a long time to live in fretful impatience, waiting for revolt.

Three weeks passed without incident, and the officers and crew became lulled. Then, one day, a squall came up from what seemed to be a cloudless sky, and the crew rushed aloft to take in sail; at the same time the slaves rose up against their masters, breaking through the gratings aft, and pouring onto the deck. In the cabin the women also took this chance to try to seize their freedom.

In a moment, forty Africans were on deck, brandishing barrel staves from broken water casks or billets of wood that they had been given as pillows. Captain Canot wrote:

> The blow that prostrated the first white man was the earliest symptom I detected of the revolt, but in an instant I had the

arm-chest open on the quarter deck and the mate and steward beside me to protect it. Matters, however, did not stand so well forward of the mainmast. Four of the hands were disabled by clubs, while the rest defended themselves and the wounded as well as they could with handspikes or whatever could suddenly be clutched. I had always charged the cook, on such an emergency, to distribute from his coppers a liberal supply of scalding water upon the belligerents; and, at the first sign of revolt he endeavored to baptize the heathen with his steaming slush. But dinner had been over for some time, so that the lukewarm liquid only irritated the savages, one of whom laid the unfortunate "doctor" bleeding in the scuppers.

The captain's next move was to pass out guns and tell his comrades to aim low and fire:

> The guns were loaded with buckshot, to suit such an occasion, so that the first two discharges brought several of the rebels to their knees. Still, the unharmed neither fled nor ceased brandishing their weapons. Two more discharges drove them forward amongst the mass of my crew, who had retreated toward the bowsprit; but being reinforced by the boatswain and the carpenter, we took command of the hatches so effectually that a dozen additional discharges among the ebony legs drove the refractory to their quarters below.

During the fracas the vessel had gone out of control. Sails were flapping, and blocks were banging against the yards and masts. The ship was turning broadside on and was threatened by the sea and wind. But when the blacks were put down, the crew rushed to right affairs.

The issue was not yet settled. The Negroes in the hold were driven down but not out of fight. They could not come up, but the slavers could not go down.

The women were taken out of the cabin under guard and kept on deck. Several boards were taken from the bulkhead that separated the cabin from the hold, and a party entered on

hands and knees, carrying weapons, to press the mutineers forward toward the bulkhead of the forecastle. Captain Canot
continued:

> By this time, our lamed cook had rekindled his fires, and the
> water was once more boiling. The hatches were kept open but
> guarded and all who did not fight were suffered to come singly
> on deck where they were tied. As only about sixty remained below
> engaged in conflict or defying my party of sappers and miners, I
> ordered a number of augur holes to be bored in the deck, as the
> scoundrels were forced forward near the forecastle, when a few
> buckets of boiling water rained on them through the fresh aper-
> tures brought the majority to submission. Still, however, two of the
> most savage held out against water as well as fire. I strove as long
> as possible to save their lives, but their resistance was so pro-
> longed and perilous that we were obliged to disarm them forever
> by a couple of pistol shots.
> So ended the sad revolt of *La Estrella,* in which two of my men
> were seriously wounded, while twenty-eight balls and buck shot
> were extracted with sailors' skill from the lower limbs of the slaves.
> One woman and three men perished of blows received in the
> conflict, but none were deliberately slain except the two men,
> who resisted unto death.[10]

That journey was fraught with trouble. A few days later,
on the way to Puerto Rico, the captain discovered that one
slave, a youngster he had been using as a cabin boy, had
come down with smallpox. When he discovered that no others
were infected, the captain gave the boy poison and threw the
body over the side. But the voyage ended unhappily for the
captain; he was chased by a British corvette off Cape Maize
and was forced to run into the Cuban shore, beach the schooner,
and save the cargo. He managed to save half, perhaps two-
thirds, of the slaves. Then the British ship sent its boats to
board the broken hulk of *La Estrella.* The British burned the
ship to be sure that it did not again sail into those waters as a
slaver.

These were the elements of slaving in the year 1839: conscience-stricken and conscientious British naval vessels out to stop the slave trade; conscienceless men of all nationalities out to perpetuate the trade and make fortunes for themselves. The market existed — and only a fool believed it was the Cuban market although nearly all cargoes of slaves were sent to Cuba. The market was across the Caribbean on the southern shores of the United States, where the planters had an insatiable need for new slave labor to increase their plantings.

New England had its share of the loot and had to take its share of the blame. No one in the United States knew this better than the wise men of the North.

In the North the issue of slavery was affected by the Puritanism of the New Englanders. They were part of the triangular trade pattern in slaves and rum and manufactures and they supplied the bottoms that supported the Africa-Cuba slave trade.

All the facts were known in the summer of 1839 when a drama began in the haciendas of the government offices of Havana and in the great *barracoon* of that slave market.

2/Havana *Barracoon*

It was common knowledge along the African coast that Don Pedro Blanco was the king of the slavers. Until 1820 the west coast of Africa had been open for slavery all along the fifteen-hundred-mile stretch from the Rio Gambia to Cape Palmas, with a break at the port of Sierra Leone, which served as the principal point of departure and trade in everything but slaves.

In 1821 the American Colonization Society purchased lands at Monrovia, and began to buy more and more until it was possible to establish a black African republic, which the society called Liberia. Because this project was looked upon with favor by the leaders of all European nations and the United States, the slavers were careful not to try to work the Liberian country, but they worked around it. By 1824 the slave trade on the windward coast north and west of Cape Palmas was confined largely to Portuguese settlements. Principal among them was the region around the Gallinas River, a sluggish stream, sometimes green and sometimes brown-yellow, that idles through the malarial swamps on its way to the Atlantic Ocean. The Gallinas opens out into a bay or lagoon before the fresh water becomes entirely salt, and a harbor protected by a sandbar was formed there thousands of years ago by the silt of the river.

Here was Lomboko, first among the slave centers of Africa, and here in 1824 came Don Pedro Blanco, a swarthy, thin Spanish gentleman who was to spend the next fifteen years on the slave coast and then leave it to go to Havana and become a millionaire.[1]

Don Pedro was an educated man, a sea captain from Malaga in Spain, who had come to the Gallinas River originally as captain of a slave ship. On his first voyage he had difficulty in obtaining slaves, and had sent his ship back under the command of the mate with barely a hundred slaves aboard — just enough to pay expenses. Don Pedro had remained, for he had seen that the shortage of slaves was simply a matter of logistics. There was a demand. There was a supply, an endless supply, given the cupidity of African chiefs and the endless wars and feuds among tribes. What was needed was a middleman who could secure the supply to meet the demand and keep the slaves in a central location until they were called for by slaving captains.

Thus began Don Pedro's empire. From the cargo of his ship the *Conquistador* he kept some cloth, some silver and gold coins, tobacco, and a large supply of rum, and with these trading goods he made himself known as the most liberal and amenable slave trader on the west coast of Africa. In four short years he had repaid the owners of the *Conquistador* all he owed and was in business for himself. In fifteen years he was the wealthiest man on the coast, wealthy enough to return to civilized life and leave his vast holdings in the hands of subordinates. Under the vigilant eye of the British navy, trade was diminishing until by 1839, it was sufficient if one ship out of three reached Havana and sold its cargo. By this time Don Pedro did not need the money and the wear and tear on nerves was too great.

Also, his establishment on the Gallinas River was imposing, consisting of a dozen small islets in the lagoon. He lived on one island in splendor and kept a seraglio on another. Other isles were made into *barracoons,* a dozen of them holding from a hundred to five hundred slaves each.

The *barracoons* were much like the American forts of the frontier West, although designed to serve exactly the opposite purpose. The American forts were built to keep the natives out; these stockades were built to keep the natives in, built of rough-hewn trees four to six inches in diameter, driven five feet into the ground and clamped together with double rows of iron bars. The roofs of the big central houses were built of the same poles, overlaid with thatch of the wiry elephant grass of the region or with reeds. The *barracoons* were constructed with entrances at each end of the long houses, so that they could be adequately guarded by a few men armed with muskets and cutlasses.

Don Pedro became so powerful that he refused to do business with any slaver or supplier who did not come to him first. His fortune was derived from the huge difference between the price of a slave purchased from an African princeling or captor and the price of a slave sold at the *barracoon* in Havana. The trade in *bars* was very tricky: at this time the *bar* equalled a half-dollar in silver, but it also equalled a pound and a half of tobacco, a six-foot length of cotton cloth, a pound of powder; and a dozen bars bought a musket. Thus the trade could be very complicated and even more lucrative than it appeared on the surface. Theoretically, a male slave sold for a hundred *bars,* but by trading in goods, the slaver might buy him for $12 to $18 and then sell him in the market at Havana for $450, a 3,000 percent profit.

In the spring of 1839, a stream of slaves, bound for the New World began arriving at the *barracoons* at Lomboko. They came chained, bound, roped, or even drugged, brought by foot and by canoe, and sometimes by caravan which also traded in salt and hides and ivory.[2]

One day a young man named Singbe came stumbling into the *barracoons* of Don Pedro Blanco. Singbe was about twenty-

five years old, a powerful youth of middle size, with a strong
nose and high forehead, slightly thickened lips, and a curly,
woolly thatch of hair on his head. A native of the farming village
of Mani in the Dzhopoa district of the land of the Mendis,
which lay about ten days' march into the interior, he was a
subject of King Kalumbo who lived at Kawmendi. Singbe was
a hardworking rice planter who lived with his father and his
wife, son and two daughters.

One morning Singbe left his cone-shaped hut, setting out for
his rice field, when he was accosted by four men and taken
captive. His right hand was tied to his neck so that he could
neither deliver a blow nor run fast, and he was prodded along
the trail to the village of Mayagilalo, the leader of the men
who had captured him. Mayagilalo needed some one like
Singbe to pay a debt; it was an immutable law of the tribal
Africans that debts had to be paid. If a man could pay no
other way he would go into slavery to satisfy his creditor.
One way out for Mayagilalo was to capture some other man
and sell him into slavery.

Three days later Mayagilalo handed Singbe over to Bamadha,
son of Shaka, king of the Genduma of the Vai country, which
was the territory of Don Pedro Blanco. Shaka and his tribes-
men had often dealt with Don Pedro, for they had developed
a taste for rum and wanted muskets, powder, and shot both
for hunting and making war on their many enemies.

For a month Singbe was kept in the village of the king of
the Genduma, and then he and other captives were brought
to Lomboko, where they were thrust into one of the *barracoons*.
So for rum and guns and bolts of cloth, Singbe and his com-
patriots were sold into the white man's slavery.

Day after day the *barracoons* filled up. Another to come
was Gilabaru, an older man, also a Mendi but from the country
of the Mandingo, where men spoke Arabic as well as their native
tongues and learned language, literature and religion all in one
as they wrote the verses of the Koran from right to left. Gila-

baru was much shorter than Singbe — only about four-feet-eleven — and from a different and more sophisticated culture in the deep interior, a distance of two months march up the river valleys of the West Africa country.

Gilabaru wore a mustache and beard, unlike the clean-shaven Singbe. He, too, was the victim of chance: his uncle had purchased two slaves in Bandi and had given them in payment of an old debt. One of the slaves ran away, and in retaliation Gilabaru was siezed by the creditor as he was traveling on the road to Taurang in the Bandi country. He was then brought to Lomboko.

And there was Kimbo, also mustachioed and bearded, who was sold into slavery by his own king in the Bullom country and sold in turn to a Spaniard who brought him down the river to the slave pens. There was Nazha-ulu, a man different from the others, with prognathous jaw and buck teeth filed quite sharp. It was said that he was a cannibal from the Congo. He could not readily communicate, although he spoke Mandingo, a language well known to the whites through the works of missionaries.

There was Burna, a blacksmith; and Gbatu, a much tattoed nobleman; Gnakwoi, a Balu who did not speak Mendi; Kwong, who was born at Mambuli, and who like Burna had been caught with another man's wife. In almost every kingdom of West Africa, adultery was punishable by enslavement, the adulterous male becoming the slave of the man he had wronged, and that is how Burna and Kwong entered captivity.

Fuliwa, a Mendi from Mano, became a slave in quite another fashion not uncommon in this fierce country. His village was surrounded by enemies one night, and after a bloody battle, the survivors were captured and sold to the Spanish slavers. There were father and son, Pie and Fuliwulu, members of the Timmani tribe who were celebrated as hunters. Pie claimed that he had killed five leopards and three elephants, a very impressive record for any hunter. Pugnwawni, a native of an

area east of Mendiland was sold into slavery by his maternal
uncle for a coat.

Most told the same sad story of having been about their own
business, usually on a trail or road, when they were set upon by
parties of men looking for slaves to sell to the whites. Sometimes,
as with Sessi, a slender Bandi, there was a fight. He was shot
in the leg before he was captured and enslaved. Shule, enslaved because of misconduct with the wife of Maya in the
Konabu region of the Mendi country, was walking with his
master one day when both were set upon and seized as slaves
to be sold to the Spaniards. A few, like Fang, were the sons of
noblemen. (His father was a minor king of the Mendi and he
was captured while out of his own territory.)

There were some women and a few children in the group
in Don Pedro's *barracoons*: a small boy named Kale, who was
stolen while on the trail one day, three little girls: Teme,
kidnaped along with her mother and brother and sister and
then separated from them; Kagne, sold by her father into slavery
to pay a debt; and Margru, who came into slavery in the same
way.

In the *barracoons* they were fed well on rice and oil, for it
would not have been good business to starve them. Occasionally
there was a little fish to keep them strong, a little fresh fruit,
a few vegetables. The time went slowly; the *barracoons* were
long in filling up this winter, and the slavers from the west were
long in coming. It was a full two months after Singbe's capture
before a schooner came into sight.

The schooner was quickly spotted by the watchmen who
sat in tall towers around the edges of the Gallinas river
waiting for ships, and it was quickly identified as not being one
of the British cruisers that made life so difficult for Don Pedro
and his men.[3]

The schooner, the *Tecora*, was the property of Don Pedro
Martinez and Company, of Havana, one of the wealthiest and
most notorious of the firms that dealt in slaves. The schooner

came into harbor, the slaves were quickly sold, some two hundred of them, and they were herded aboard the schooner.[4]

As slavers went, this ship was not among the worst;
Singbe and his companions had nearly four feet of headroom,
where on another ship they might have had closer to three
feet. They were chained in groups of five, stripped of every
stitch of clothing as they came aboard the schooner, and led
below decks where they were laid out in columns, one man's
head against another man's thigh.

The voyage to Cuba, their destination, took nearly three
months. Food grew short, and the slaves were put on small
rations. And when water became scarce, the ration was cut.
Many slaves died — the bloody flux broke out — but most sur-
vived.

Finally, in June, the two-masted slave schooner entered Cuban
waters, and with the first smells and sight of land the slaves
were brought up from their confinement and released from
their chains.

At night, in the safety of darkness when no British or American man-of-war would be in Cuban waters, the schooner landed
its precious cargo by small boat in a port of a village not far
from Havana, and in a few days the slaves were moved into
the *barracoon* called Misericordia, kept by Señor Riera, a long-
time business associate of the house of Martinez.[5]

At the *barracoon* the slaves were fed better and treated
better than they had been for nearly three months aboard the
slave ship. They had rice and yams and ripe bananas to eat,
and oil to anoint their cracked skins. The weather was warm
and they were neither chained nor crowded, although
they were locked inside the slave corral.

In a few days Señor Riera brought into the *barracoon* a
young Spanish dandy named Don José Ruiz, also known as Pepe
to his friends, who was seeking slaves to add to the family
estates on the island of Cuba near Puerto Principe. At least
that was what he said he was seeking: there was some reason

to believe that the slaves might disappear from the estate into the slave market at Puerto Principe, and some reason to believe that they might turn up somewhere on the southern coast of the United States.

Such quick changes had been occurring far too often in the last few months of 1838 and the early months of 1839 to please Americans who did not like slavery. One facilitating force in the brisk, if illegal, trade between the United States and Cuba was the United States Consul to Cuba, Nicholas P. Trist. Consul Trist was a Southerner, married to the granddaughter of Thomas Jefferson. He was a slavery man, and he was suspect in the dealings that occurred between Havana and any number of ports along the southern slavery coast of the United States. This year, after many rumors and much grumbling, discontent with his activities was making itself known in the public press. The New York *Journal of Commerce* complained openly that more than twenty ships had been sold to Cuban firms with the full knowledge that they would be used in the slave trade. Most annoying and humiliating of all these sales was the transfer of the former United States Revenue Cutter *Campbell* to hands that would use it in the slave trade it had been built to stamp out. For the first time Consul Trist was castigated publicly in print.[6] It did no good, however, for Trist was a good Democrat, as was President Van Buren, and there was no upsetting of the delicate balance that held the Democratic party in power in several states of the South.

Whatever his actual intentions were regarding the slaves of the Misericordia *barracoon,* Don José Ruiz need not reveal them insofar as Governor General Ezpeleta of Cuba was concerned. The Governor General understood the problem of slavery very well. His understanding was heightened by the $15 per head that he took for every slave transferred among the Cuban islands.

On June 26 Don José arrived at the *barracoon.* With the practiced eye and hand of a slave dealer he went over the slaves, seeking some fifty of them. He looked in their eyes, opened their mouths, and checked their nostrils. He examined them for venereal disease and anal problems. He thumped them and thwacked them with the practice of long experience of a man dealing in human flesh. He picked out forty-nine of the captives, young and middle-aged, and bought them from the slavers at $450 each, investing $22,000. If he intended to take them to the plantation to work the sugar cane, they would be worth the price. If he intended to take them to the slave market to be transshipped to the United States, they might be worth twice as much.[7]

Following the purchase there were a few formalities. A call must be made at the office of Governor General Ezpeleta to regularize the proceedings. In the treaty of 1820 between Spain and England, Great Britain had paid Spain 400,000 pounds as indemnification for lost slaves, and had then demanded that the slave trade be ended. The Spanish crown had agreed that no more slaves would be imported into Spanish territory, but the agreement meant absolutely nothing in Cuba. Ezpeleta took his money and kept his eyes tightly closed. Don José Ruiz went to the governor's office and soon returned with a document, a *traspasso*, which asserted that he was the owner of forty-nine Negro slaves, called *ladinos*, which meant they had been in residence in Cuba since before 1820, and that Don José was permitted to transport them by ship to Puerto Principe. The *traspasso* bore the unmistakable scrawl of Governor General Ezpeleta himself.[8]

That night the slave dealer's guards brought out their chains and iron collars again. The men were chained together in groups, they were given Christian names for use on the *traspasso* (Singbe became Joseph Cinquez), they were given loincloths, and after one more meal they were marched through the dark streets of Havana to the docks. Then they were marched onto the decks of a schooner and put into the hold.

Don José met Don Pedro Montes, another Spanish gentleman

on his way to Port Principe, who had purchased the little boy
Kale, and the three little girls, Teme, Kague, and Margru. He
conferred with Captain Ramon Ferrer, the master of this coasting schooner of 120 tons. They decided that it would not be
necessary to chain the captives, for they would be only a few
days in their crossing and no trouble was expected.

It was a dark night, and the slaves did not know anything
about the ship they had boarded. It would have meant nothing
to them anyway, to learn that it was the *Amistad,* the Spanish
translation of the original American name of this American-built
ship, which had once been called *Friendship.*

3/The Long Black Schooner

The *Amistad* was swift and tidy, built for speed in the shipyards at Baltimore. She was what was called a clipper-built schooner, one of the latest of a long line of proud ships that were always suspect by naval officers in those days because they were built specifically to meet the needs of the slave trade.

The *Amistad* was already loaded when Señor Ruiz and Señor Montes agreed with Captain Ramon Ferrer on a price for the shipment of the slaves to Principe. The ship carried a full cargo of crockery, copper plate, silks and satins and other luxury goods. Her owner had the cargo insured for $40,000. Don José Ruiz added $20,000 more in insurance on his human cargo, and Don Pedro Montes insured his four young slaves for about $1,300. All this was done on the day after the slaves were loaded, as the *Amistad* sat in Havana harbor under the guns of the great fortress, the Morro Castle. Since Captain Ferrer was sole owner, he could decide when and where he would travel. The crew consisted of two slaves and two sailors. One of the slaves cooked for passengers, the slave cargo, and the crew. The other ran errands for the captain and served as cabin boy.

Celestino, the mulatto slave, might have been the son of the captain: he seemed to have many of that gentleman's features, although he was very dark. As cook, it was his job to prepare the huge cauldrons of rice and boiled potatoes that the slaves would eat. He was also in charge of their water supply.

On the morning of June 27 the slaves were brought up ten at a time to eat their morning meal in the warm sun of Havana harbor. Then they were marched forward where the water was kept in casks, and were given water in tin cups by one of the sailors. For half an hour or so the slaves were allowed to stay on deck, under careful watch as they exercised.

When tide and wind were right that day, the *Amistad* was made ready for sea. The slaves were safely stowed below decks, out of sight so that no interest would be aroused in the minds of British or United States cruisers in these waters. According to the *traspassos,* all was in order, for they detailed quite correctly the number of slaves belonging to Don José and to Don Pedro. They said, of course, that all these slaves had been in Cuba for nineteen years. In the case of several of the young men, this meant they had come to Cuba before they were born. In the case of the four child slaves of Don Pedro, there was not even any possibility of explaining away the difference between the words and facts.

Yet on June 27, when the customs and port officials clambered aboard the long black schooner, they saw nothing amiss. The *traspassos* were all in order, were they not? They were signed by the Governor General himself, were they not? If they called the three little girls (not one of them over twelve years old) "adult" *ladinos,* well, that was just one of those small government matters that any man of the world had come to accept.

In the afternoon, when the *Amistad* reached the edge of the harbor, she was checked by the guard ship and lastly by officials from Morro Castle. Then she moved out into the roadstead past the castle and dropped anchor. Here there was little danger that the slaves might try to get away. The slaves slept below deck. The captain slept on a mattress on deck, for his cabin was too warm, and the passengers slept on deck as well. Tomorrow, on the tide, they would sail for Puerto Principe, 300 miles from Havana.

And at dawn on June 28 the *Amistad* did sail, full canvas quickly run up the two masts, the jib, and the flying gaff. Under way it was a sleek ship, masts raked back raffishly, with an extra-long bowsprit capable of carrying two and three jibs. This fore- and aft-rigging, with a single yard on foremast, and mainmast made the *Amistad* ideal for the coastal waters of the Caribbean. It could thread through the islands safely, not worrying about the sudden buffs from shore or the sudden switches in wind that killed the way of a full-rigged ship. The topsails gave the extra power that a captain always liked when there was a following wind, but he could sail very nicely on either tack. Captain Ferrer had a fresh breeze, and he did not expect it to take more than two days and one night to reach Puerto Principe, whereupon he would be rid of this unpleasant human cargo that left so definite an odor in his vessel.

Soon Cuba was a low blot on the horizon. It was to remain in sight, for Captain Ferrer was no fool. It was early for hurricanes, but tropical storms could come up on a moment's notice, and he preferred to do his coasting well within sight of land, preferably not more than eighteen or twenty miles off shore, so that he could run in if the skies began to blacken.[1]

His luck was foul on this trip, and he soon found himself sailing tack and tack. Unless the wind changed it might take a week to reach Puerto Principle.

But since there was nothing to be done, captain and crew settled down to the quiet, regular life of coasting. The sun was bright and the weather was good enough, even if the winds were adverse. There was nothing to worry about. All they had to lose was time. It was true that they did not carry provisions for more than four or five days for the slaves, but this would have to be made up by cutting back on the blacks' food and water.

So it was. Not knowing how long they might be at sea, the captain ordered the slaves' food reduced. He could have run into port anywhere, but this would have meant additional contact with the Spanish bureaucracy, and the captain would have had to pay the expenses. The two slave-owners had contracted for a trip to Puerto Principe. It was the captain's responsibility to get them there without further charge.

On the second day out the blacks began to grumble when their food was cut. Two of the slaves went to the water cask on the deck without permission, and when the crew members caught them at it, Captain Ferrer thrashed them with his cat.[2] Then the wounds were treated in the sailor's way, rubbed with salt, gunpowder, and rum. For a hundred years and more this had been the traditional preventative against infection at sea. The scars were large and hard, but the treatment was usually effective, painful as it might be.

On the second day the wind continued to blow against them, and again on the third and fourth days. The *Amistad* was sailing close to shore, and would continue. The captain was worried about the blacks, but not enough to interrupt his voyage.

On that fourth day the slaves began to talk a little to Celestino, Captain Ferrer's mulatto slave. What would happen to them when they reached their destination? they asked.

Celestino was cursed with the soul of a *mestizo*, called inferior by the white men whose culture he had adopted, and able to satisfy his feelings of inferiority only by lording it over those beneath him.

The white men would eat them, he told the slaves.

(No greater error has ever been committed aboard a slave ship.)

On hearing this frightening news, the Negroes began to talk among themselves. Not all of them could converse with any fluidity, but they were able to make themselves understood. Most of the slaves were Mendis, which meant that their languages bore some relationship to each other. Among the Mendis the leader was Singbe, the strongest and brightest of the younger men. He began to make a plan.

Singbe had quickly realized that on the voyage across the Atlantic the *Tecora* had sailed west. Would it not, then, be possible to return to Africa by sailing east? There were forty-nine slaves, three white masters, two white crew members, and the two black slaves of the captain. What these two blacks would do was not known and not important. The captain was armed with cutlass and pistol, the two slave masters were armed with pistols, and the crewmen were armed with knives. But to offset this the slaves had discovered among the cargo being taken to Puerto Principe a number of cane knives, terrible, strong machete-type blades with wide square ends tapering down to narrow edges at the handle, eminently suitable for chopping hollow cane — and for chopping heads.

On the fifth night, after their evening meal, the slaves quieted down, even though badly fed and given insufficient water. The captain, who had grown exceedingly nervous, was lulled into believing that they were somehow content, and at midnight he lay down in the cool of the night on his mattress on deck, his mulatto Celestino by his side.

The slaves came out of their hold, waking Don José Ruiz, who threatened them. But they were armed and not willing to listen to his threats. In a few moments they gained the deck, seized him, and reached the place where the captain lay asleep.

Singbe struck the first blow. He wounded the captain slightly, but Captain Ferrer dodged and was saved for the moment. Celestino was not so lucky. Singbe's second blow nearly severed the mulatto's head. The captain retreated, Singbe after him. He drew his sword and fought back.

As the unequal battle raged on deck the two Spanish sailors retreated. The helmsman left the wheel, and joined his companion. Swiftly and silently they lowered the stern boat, clambered into it, and cut themselves loose from the *Amistad*.

In a moment they were gone, heading for the safety of the land, which was about eighteen miles away.

Singbe and several of the others kept fighting with the captain until one great blow of Singbe's cane knife smashed through Captain Ferrer's skull and he fell to the deck, bleeding, his life running out. Singbe proposed to kill all the white men, but wiser heads — Gilabaru, Shule, and others — reminded him that alone they could not sail the ship back to Africa. He wanted to kill the black slave Antonio, too, the captain's boy, but they reminded him that Antonio was their one contact with the whites. He could speak a little of the languages of Africa that they understood, and he could also speak Spanish.

It was decided that the whites and the black boy would be preserved. The slaves held Ruiz and promised him that if he was quiet he would not be hurt. He did not move. Don Pedro Montes, however, was less inclined to believe them. He had armed himself with a stick and a knife and now he struck at the blacks as they tried to seize him. They struck back with their knives, wounding him. Don Pedro ran below to hide from his attackers. He found a place between two barrels and wrapped himself in a sail. One of the blacks went after him with a knife, but another slave intervened, and Don Pedro's life was saved, although he was hustled out of the hold and back on deck.

Don Pedro had once been a ship captain and he knew navigation, although he did not have charts that would take him to Sierra Leone or the coast of West Africa. That was the intent of the Africans. Singbe, speaking through the slave Antonio, told Don Pedro that he would most certainly be killed if he did not help them get back to Africa. Don Pedro was already a sorry sight, wounded in head and arm and expecting to be murdered at any moment. He agreed because there was nothing to do but agree, and the ship was turned again to the east, to head straight for the rising sun. That way, said Singbe, lay home.

The Africans set about cleaning up the ship and making ready for the trip. They dragged the bodies of Captain Ferrer and Celestino the slave to the rail and threw them over. They did the same with the bodies of the two men killed by the captain in his fight for life. Then they set sail, setting only the third jib sail and the fore and main tops, furling the rest, perhaps in the theory that the jib would carry them on tacks and the topsail would catch the following winds.

The Africans were not in any way a disciplined group, and Singbe's authority over them was extremely limited. They accepted him as leader, but this did not keep them from demanding their "rights" as newly freed men. They broke into the casks of beef and water on deck and satiated themselves. They cooked the beef and rice and plantains they found in Celestino's galley, and stuffed themselves. Then they went below and began to ransack the cargo. They found four muskets and gave them to the men who knew how to use them, like Pie the hunter.

For several hours the *Amistad* ran with the winds, her wheel spinning this way and that, as the Africans celebrated their victory and the winning of freedom. Meanwhile Antonio and the two white men stood by, grim-faced, frightened, not knowing when they might be killed.

Singbe tried to keep his men under control, but it was impossible. Soon those who had gone below emerged on deck, carrying bottles and boxes. They had found raisins in the cargo, and solid and liquid medicines, and wines. They ate the raisins and the medicines and drank the wines. Many of the Africans were soon drunk and slumped about the deck. Many became sick from the mixture. Several died.[3]

While the new crewmen gorged themselves, Singbe recaptured his authority. He found a pair of white pantaloons, which he put on, and he fixed the captain's sword in his bandolier. In ransacking the captain's cabin he had found $8,000 in Spanish doubloons, the captain's private fortune. If they made their way back to Africa he would be a wealthy man.[4]

Then began as strange a voyage as was ever sailed on the seven seas. Singbe brought Don José and Don Pedro to the helm and explained that they must sail the ship back to Africa or they would both be killed. It did not take the white men long to catch on. Singbe sent his men aloft to unfurl the canvas, but they had no experience as sailors; their lines were slack and the canvas would not do their bidding. They could manage the jib and the topsails; the others they could scarcely decipher, and after a few misguided attempts to clew up the main and other sails, they gave up.

By day Singbe insisted that they steer east. At first he could not understand the need for tacking, but he soon learned, and did not become so suspicious when Don Pedro steered the ship first on one tack and then on the other. The Spaniards had determined to keep the ship in the Antilles or that general area, hoping to be discovered by a friendly ship. Don Pedro considered turning the ship around, but he was threatened constantly with death and knew that if Singbe awoke some morning to find the rising sun over his shoulder, he might murder them.

Between them, Don Pedro and Don José managed to keep the ship from sailing out into the broad reaches of the Atlantic. They were helped by the Africans' lack of knowledge. Soon the main yard was gone, the jib was in shreds, and the only effective sail was the foretop. Day in and day out they boxed the compass, for Don Pedro steered as close to due east as possible when the grim figure of Singbe was standing at his side, and in storm or darkness he turned to steer north or west.

For a time they sailed in the Old Bahama Channel. Then slowly they began working northward. When they encountered storms the superstitious Africans cowered in the rain, afraid they would be drowned. When the sun shone they pointed east and hoped they soon would be home.

Here and there they stopped at a small island or key and filled their water casks. June had passed into July before the slave revolt, and July now waned. The bottom grew green with fouling and the ship slowed. The sails rotted and flapped against the masts. The food supplies grew slimmer and slimmer, with Singbe carefully doling out the daily rations. The Africans became restless and depressed. Half a dozen died of sickness or from the effects of eating medicine.

July drifted into August...

They stopped at St. Andrews Island for water and met no one. They steered for New Providence, but when they approached the island, the Negroes decided it might be dangerous to land because they could be captured and enslaved. They vowed that they would rather die than become slaves again.

Soon a total of ten of the Negroes were dead, and Singbe doubled his precautions. He placed a guard on the cargo and insisted that nothing be eaten except what he handed out.

So the *Amistad* zig-zagged up the eastern coast of the United States, out of sight of land, steering north northeast in the daytime and west at night.[5] They began to encounter other vessels.

By this time the Africans and their white captives were in a sorry state. They were nearly out of water, and some of the blacks began drinking salt water, which made them ill.

Now the pilot boat *Blossom* appeared to examine this strange, almost derelict schooner, to fall in with the *Amistad* off the Woodlands, not far from the entrance to New York's harbor. The captain and crew of the *Blossom* grew suspicious when they approached the ship, saw its condition, saw that it was manned by blacks.

As the *Blossom* came alongside, Singbe sent the two whites below so they would not be seen. Through his glass, the captain of the *Blossom* saw that he had twenty-five or thirty blacks to deal with and he suspected that the ship was a slaver whose slaves had risen and probably murdered captain and crew.

Through Antonio, the former cabin boy, the *Amistad* Negroes made it clear that they needed food and water. The *Blossom* passed over both bread and water for the Negroes, which they devoured.

The *Blossom* stood by all night as *Amistad* sailed its senseless course, and the next day the *Blossom*'s captain took the slaver in tow, intending to bring her into harbor and safety.

But the Negroes made an attempt to board the *Blossom*. Seeing their knives and swords, the master of the pilot boat became frightened and cut the tow rope. The last he saw of the *Amistad*, it was riding with the wind thirty miles south-southeast of the Hook.

Putting on all the sail his pilot boat could manage, the captain sped back to New York harbor and told his strange story to the Collector of Customs, who was in charge of the port for the federal authorities. The collector immediately dispatched an armed revenue cutter manned by Coast Guardsmen to try to find the black ship with its black crew. Word was sent to the commander of the naval forces in the region, and a watch was placed at sea. The collector at Boston was alerted that there was a possible pirate vessel in the area, and the United States steam frigate *Fulton* was ordered from New York harbor in pursuit of the mystery ship.

The *Amistad*'s appearance created considerable interest among newspapers of the East Coast, largely because of the attempt by the Negroes to board the *Blossom*.[6] More sightings were reported, by the Boston *Atlas*, the New London *Gazette*, the New York *Commercial Advertiser*. The people of Greenport, Sag Harbor, and New London became anxious. Captains dared not take their coasting schooners out of port, for fear they would be trapped by the "pirate."[7]

On August 24, Captain Nock of the packet schooner *President* arrived in Norfolk, after having heard a weird tale from the captain of the schooner *Emmaline*, that indicated foul play and piracy on the high seas.

On August 20, said the captain of the *Emmaline*, he had

spotted a long, low, black schooner 75 miles off Egg Harbor. The sails were in tatters, it was flying only the foretopsail, and the bottom, painted green, was in terrible condition.

"They were out of water, and had to drink salt water for several days previously," Captain Nock said. "When the captain of the *Emmaline* boarded her, he found 25 persons on deck and a large number in the hold, apparently in a state of starvation, all black men, none of whom could speak English."

Like the *Blossom*, the *Emmaline* had attempted to take the *Amistad* in tow, but Singbe obviously feared again that they would be enslaved and made preparations to capture the new ship. Sensing the threat, the captain of the *Emmaline* cast off the tow, losing his cable but saving his ship with its crew of seven from the superior force against him.

After the tow was cast off the *Amistad* sent a boat filled with armed men alongside the *Emmaline*, but the crew of the latter lined the bulwarks and conspicuously showed the blacks their weapons.

Conversing in Spanish with Antonio, the captain of the *Emmaline* answered the Negroes' requests for food and water. If they would go back to their ship and produce their papers for him, and if those papers showed that the ship was on a legitimate voyage, then the *Emmaline* would give them assistance, the captain promised.

As the crew from the *Amistad* returned to the schooner, the *Emmaline*'s men caught sight of a white man coming up from below. Singbe had allowed Don Pedro on deck to ask advice. It was apparent what Don Pedro's advice must have been, for the blacks hoisted their boat aboard the *Amistad* and made no further attempt to board the *Emmaline*.

Next morning the *Emmaline* was still in sight of the black schooner, although not within hailing distance. The Negroes fired three guns at the ship. No balls struck the *Emmaline*, but the captain, obviously alarmed, changed course to avoid the long black schooner. The *Emmaline* did not see the *Amistad* again.[9]

This account was similar to that of the schooner *Eveline*, traveling from New Bedford to Wilmington under Captain Sears. He encountered the *Amistad* in the same vicinity, and from signs he understood that they needed water. He boarded the ship and found the decks littered with broken crockery, umbrellas, looking glasses, and other remains of cargo. He was told that the ship had been out about three months, and that all the white men, captain and crew, had been washed overboard in a storm. No one aboard spoke English.

But after he took her in tow, and had towed her until dark, he heard a voice in English telling the men to make sail, get alongside the *Eveline* and take sails and water. Captain Sears became frightened and cut his tow, leaving a water cask aboard the *Amistad*.[10]

Rumors raced up and down the coast. It had been known for several weeks that two men from a schooner had made their way ashore in Cuba and told the tale of the massacre of captain and passengers in an uprising of a cargo of slaves. Captain Sears warned the captain of the revenue cutter *Gallatin*, saying this must be the same ship. The sea watch was doubled.

The situation of the Negroes aboard the *Amistad* was growing desperate. They did not know whether they would find freedom or slavery if they landed. They were afraid to engage other ships and they were afraid not to. Their attitude was a combination of hostility and humility, but while the hostility showed, the humility did not, and the ships they saw either gave them a wide berth or veered off to report their presence to the authorities.

Don Pedro led the black schooner up and down the coast of Long Island, hoping that some official United States vessel would capture them, for his worries about property were less than his worries about his life, and as the blacks grew desperate

Singbe grew more irritated with this pilot who had not led them back to Africa after all.

Near the end of August, Captain Seaman of the pilot boat *Gratitude* encountered the *Amistad* and reported to the *Columbian Centinel* of Boston:

> She spoke the long, low, black schooner twenty-five miles East of Fire Island and about eighteen miles from the land, standing E.N.E. The *Gratitude* ran within a few yards of her with the intention of putting a pilot aboard. Two or three of the blacks, who appeared to be the ringleaders and who kept the others in awe, made signs to the pilot not to come. One had a pistol in one hand and a cutlass in the other, which he flourished over his head to keep the others down. These appeared to be very anxious to receive a pilot and when the eye of the fellow who had the pistol was aft of them, they would beckon the pilot to come aboard. The schooner had a name on her stern which they took to be the *Almeda*. She had a small gilt eaglehead. The latest news from the suspicious vessel is that on Saturday at sunset she was off the end of Long Island, Montauk Point, North by East, twenty miles distant. She was standing east with what sail she was able to make.[11]

So the struggle went on. Each day Singbe put his pistol at the head of Don Pedro and told him to steer east. Each night Don Pedro or Don José turned the ship west or north again, and let the winds blow her back upon the land.

They saw many ships, but Singbe became less and less inclined to use reason as hope failed all of them. Pilot Boat No. 3 out of New York pulled alongside and gave them some apples when the Negroes indicated they needed food. Pilot Boat No. 4 came alongside too, but Singbe waved them away, and the pilot boat left with no more contact than that.

Whenever the *Amistad* neared another ship, Singbe stationed himself next to Don José Ruiz, the only man aboard who spoke English, and threatened to kill him if he made a false move.[12]

Once Don Pedro recognized that they were off Montauk light and attempted to run the ship aground, but the ship drifted off with the tide. It seemed that the *Amistad* was fated to drift and blow along the United States coast forever, seen but avoided, and unseen by any authorities who could make some disposition of the ship. Singbe was as dispiritied as the whites; he no longer expected to get home to Africa. He no longer expected anything. He stayed in command because there was nothing else to do.

4/Capture

In New York, Boston, Philadelphia, and all ports between, terror struck the men of the sailing ships when they learned of the continued presence off shore of the long, low, black schooner filled with Negroes. There had been too many tales of slave mutinies, too many tales of piracy, and even of cannibalism, and they were aroused. A cry went up, capture the pirates before they threatened the commerce of the whole Northeast.

On August 24 the *Amistad* anchored, for perhaps the thirtieth time, off Culloden Point on the edge of Fort Pond Bay on the eastern end of Long Island, between Gardner's Point and Montauk Point. Singbe intended to send men ashore and, with the captain's gold, to buy enough supplies to make the final attempt to reach Africa. He would sail due east as long as they could sail.

This was settled country, potato land and fisherman's land. Sag Harbor was one of the famous fishing and whaling ports of the nation. There were many people not far from shore to see the lines of the black schooner, and people who could tell by the way it lay, main topyard torn away, knew that it had run into heavy weather and was badly in need of a refit. Such vessels were rare in these waters; vessels that did not pull openly into a major port were rare and suspicious.

The next morning the suspicions increased when a boatload of naked blacks rowed ashore, bearing trade goods and gold. The people refused to speak to these naked savages, who might be pirates, or even cannibals! Whatever they were, the modest women of Long Island closed and barred their doors. Singbe's men returned to the schooner with a full load of water and a few potatoes, but none of the chickens and pigs and other food that they had hoped to get.

On the morning of August 26 Singbe himself went ashore, desperate for provisions. If he could not buy chickens and pigs, what about dogs? He had the captain's wealth with him, a money belt filled with gold doubloons, and he paid for dogs at the rate of three doubloons each, a price of about $45, at which most islanders would sell any animal in their possession.

Word of the maneuvers of the strange vessel on August 25 was not long in reaching Sag Harbor, the home of so many ship captains. Ashore that day were Captain Henry Green and Captain Pelatiah Fordham. On August 26 they drove to the Culloden Point area to take a look.

Singbe and his foragers were having some success ashore. They obtained gin, a few loaves of bread, and meat. They found corn. They encountered Captains Green and Fordham with a group of whites, all of them armed. They scattered to hide, but were stopped by the white men.

"What country is this?" asked one of the Negroes who spoke broken English.

"This is America," Captain Green replied.

"Is it a slave country?" the Negro asked.

"No, it is a free country."[1]

The Negroes then gave Green and the others presents that they had stripped from their ship's cargo. They handed over their weapons; even Singbe gave up his gun and sword.

The Negroes parleyed and traded with the Americans for some time. The whites were very much interested in the blacks' money, and considered capturing the ship and turning it in for salvage, which would have made them all wealthy. But Singbe was not easily gulled, and he did not relinquish either money or command of his ship.

While the Negroes were trying to bargain with the whites to get back to Africa, a sail rose up on the horizon, on the Atlantic Ocean side of the point. Soon the hull was visible and it swiftly approached the *Amistad*'s anchorage.

The ship was the United States' surveying brig *Washington,* commanded by Lieutenant Commander Thomas R. Gedney. His special duty this August was to survey the waters by sounding between Gardner's Point and Montauk Point. He was performing his duty when he saw the black schooner, and as was everyone else who spied it, he was immediately attracted by its seabitten condition. Then when he saw the cluster of people around Captain Green's wagon, and the blacks and the anchored ship, he ordered his helmsman to stand in towards the shore and hail the schooner.

As Gedney watched, the boat that had brought the blacks ashore began moving back and forth between the ship and land. He decided he must take action, and ordered Lieutenant Richard W. Meade to board the schooner and discover her ownership, flag, and destination.

As Lieutenant Meade was rowed alongside the schooner, he saw:

> Her sides were covered with barnacles and long tentacles of seaweed streamed from her cable and her sides at the water line. Her jibs were torn and big rents and holes appeared in both foresail and mainsail as they flapped in the gentle breeze. Most of the paint was gone from her gunwales and her rail — over which coal-black African faces, fixed with a mingled curiousity and fear, peered above forms clad in the most fantastic garb. All about the deck were scattered in the most wanton and disorderly confusion parts of what evidently had been her cargo. There were rent bags of raisins, here and there half-eaten loaves of bread and various piles of silk and cotton goods. In the cabin

and hold were evidences of the same wasteful destruction. In even greater confusions, as if it had been broken into at will by a number of people, were such portions of the cargo as silks, crepes, gaudy calicoes, which had been wantonly cut and torn, many varieties of cotton and fancy fabrics, glass, hardware, books, fruits, olives, olive oil, and the heterogeneous things which a trading schooner would be likely to carry.[2]

Meanwhile, wily Captain Green was in pidgin conversation with Singbe and the others of the shore party. He discovered that they had more money aboard the *Amistad.* He instructed them to get the money, and they sent the boat back for Captain Ferrer's trunk. When the trunk arrived they did not show the money to Captain Green — Singbe was too shrewd for that — but they rattled the trunk and the captain could hear the sound of heavy bits of metal clinking inside.

As the *Washington* dispatched her boats, Captain Green was making promises to Singbe. If they would turn the money over to him, he would take care of them. They would have the provisions they needed and Captain Green would sail them back to Africa.

He had no intention of fulfilling his promises, of course; he only wanted possession of the ship so that he could claim it for salvage.

But as the discussion continued, the cutter of the *Washington* made the side of the *Amistad,* and with a hail, the United States naval contingent led by Lieutenant Meade boarded. There was no resistance. Seeing the arrival of the Americans, Singbe hastened back to the ship, with the trunk full of doubloons, and while they were busy on deck he went below into the main hatch with the trunk.

The Americans soon found Don José and Don Pedro and released them from the guard the Negroes had posted.

"These Negroes are my slaves," Don José said, "they have risen and taken the vessel; that is the leader [pointing to Singbe] and I claim your protection."[3]

Lieutenant Meade went below with Ruiz. As he was searching the vessel, Singbe dived into Captain Ferrer's trunk and filled a money belt with gold doubloons. Then he rushed to the deck and threw himself over the side.

Lieutenant Meade heard the commotion and ran to the rail. Singbe had so loaded himself with gold that he sank to the bottom, but he managed to get free of the heavy money belt, and then began swimming away from the ship. He came up about a hundred yards from the ship and saw that he was being watched. The Americans manned the cutter and began to give chase. Singbe dived and tried to escape by going around behind the stern of the ship. The Americans found him and followed.

Each time the cutter neared Singbe, he would dive, remain under water for a minute, and emerge behind the stern of the cutter. For a moment no one would see him, and then some sailor would shout a warning, and the cutter would swing around.

Singbe kept up this cat-and-mouse game for forty minutes before he realized that there was nowhere for him to go in the open water. Then he gave up and allowed the white men to pull him into the boat. As he came over the side he smiled, but he also put his hands around his neck in a gesture that clearly showed he expected to be hanged.

Lieutenant Meade took the cutter, with Singbe aboard, to the *Washington,* and there on the quarterdeck he reported the events of the last hour and a half to Lieutenant Commander Gedney.

Gedney, too, was aroused to cupidity. So many had been the sea wars, excursions against freebooters and pirates, and so great the enmity on the high seas that every seaman was well aware of the admiralty rules governing property. Gedney saw that he had a chance to become wealthy. Captain Ferrer had been sole owner of the *Amistad* and most of its cargo. Captain Ferrer was dead. *Amistad* was, for all intents and purposes, in the hands of pirates or mutineers. By seizing her, Gedney would establish a claim to the cargo and the ship. The fact that he had encountered *Amistad* as a part of his official paid duty as an officer of the United States navy did not make any difference to him. Officers were often granted salvage rights or bounty for the capture of vessels, either in time of war or against freebooters in peacetime.

Singbe, in the meantime, was wretched, certain that his end was not far off. He was returned with the rest to the *Amistad* because it was simpler to look after him with the other prisoners than to keep him in irons or in the brig of the *Washington*.

Once on deck again it was obvious who the leader of the Africans was. The men crowded around him in joy, laughing and waving their arms, embracing him. They obviously thought that they had been delivered from their enemies, and not into the hands of those who would cause them further trouble. Singbe was under no such delusion.

"Friends and brothers," Singbe told the others, "We would have returned, but the sun was against us. I would not see you serve the white man. So I induced you to help me kill the captain. I thought I should be killed. I expected it. It would have been better. You had better be killed than live many moons in misery. I shall be hanged, I think, every day. But this does not pain me. I could die happy if by dying I could save so many of my brothers from the bondage of the white men."[4]

Although handcuffed, Singbe did not give up his efforts to gain freedom. One of the Africans had died, and his body was covered with black cloth. Singbe pointed to the body and ruefully remarked that here was one of them who had found freedom.

Singbe's companions listened as he spoke of freedom and death. They became so excited, so frenzied that the Americans were sure they would try to escape. The Americans climbed the shrouds of the *Amistad* and leveled their guns at the blacks.

There was no sympathy in any American eye, for in the minds of Lieutenant Meade and Lieutenant Commander Gedney, these Africans were slaves, mutineers, murderers. They had captured a man's ship, killed him, and tried to sail away to Africa. They had imprisoned two gentlemen, Don José and Don Pedro. They had murdered a mulatto cook and threatened the cabin boy, Antonio.

At an order from Lieutenant Meade, sailors from the *Washington* grabbed Singbe again. They manacled him and hustled him over the side into the cutter of the *Washington*. In a few minutes he was back on the deck of the American naval vessel, and Gedney was being informed of the trouble brewing aboard the *Amistad*. Gedney ordered an armed guard to be maintained on the *Amistad*, and had Singbe manacled to a stay.

And constantly, from the moment Singbe was recaptured by the Americans, the Africans moaned and yelled. They continued all night Tuesday, August 26, as Gedney and his crew made the *Amistad* ready for sea. By the time Singbe had been secured it was too late to begin a voyage to an admiralty port.

Singbe was stoic. He scarcely moved and spoke less, but his mind worked all the while. On Wednesday morning he was called into the presence of Lieutenant Commander Gedney. He indicated that if the captain would let him go back aboard the *Amistad* he would show him the hiding place of Captain Ferrer's doubloons.

Gedney anxiously acceded to this request. Singbe was transferred in the cutter that morning to the *Amistad*, to the accompaniment of joyful shouts of the Africans, who watched through the gratings of the slave holds, where they had been confined once more, to preserve order.

Singbe's manacles were removed and he was taken below. The hatch was opened, he was shoved down, and the hatch was closed — but not before Antonio, the loyal slave of Captain Ferrer, was sent below to listen and report on what Singbe said to his companions.

Singbe lost no time. No sooner had he made his way into the dank hold than he began talking.

"My brothers," he said, "I am once more among you, having deceived the enemy of our race by saying I had doubloons. I come to tell you that you have only one chance for death and none for liberty. I am sure you prefer death, as I do. You can, by killing the white men now on board — and I will help you — make the people here kill you.

"It is better for you to do this, and then you will not only avert bondage yourselves, but prevent the entailment of un-numbered wrongs on your children. Come, come with me, then."

Hearing this speech delivered rapidly in Mendi, Antonio scarcely had time to shout for the Americans above before the blacks began moving toward the hatchway. In a few moments the hatch cover was off, a sea of African faces looked up into a barricade of American rifles, and Singbe was seized again and manacled. No tenderness was shown him as he was hustled off the deck of the *Amistad* back into the cutter for shipment over to the *Washington*.

As the American sailors rowed toward the *Washington*, the blacks aboard the *Amistad* whooped and howled, but Singbe did not move a muscle. He insisted on standing in the cutter and he stood quietly, his eyes fixed on the schooner.

Once aboard the brig he was taken below. He insisted, by gesture, that there was some important reason for him to be allowed above decks, and he was taken to the main deck. There he simply turned to the schooner and stared at her, not saying a word.

Captain Gedney now moved. He could not remain indefin-itely off Culloden Point; he must make some disposition of ship, passengers and the slaves who had mutinied. He could send messages to the United States courts in New York. Al-most alone among northern cities, New York contained a certain element of friendliness toward slavery. But New York state outlawed slavery. Lieutenant Commander T.R. Gedney was a sailor, not a politician. He chose a canny and direct line of action. On Wednesday evening, August 27, the commander of the *Washington* arrived in New London and sent a message to the United States Marshal at New Haven. In Connecticut, slavery was legal. The marshal immediately sought out United States District Judge A.T. Judson, and the two men headed for New London.

They arrived on Thursday morning, August 28. Judge Judson decided to hold his court of inquiry aboard the *Washington,* within a few cable lengths of the *Amistad.* What was to be decided at this point was the status of the ship, the passengers, the crew, and the cargo. Were there grounds for a trial for piracy? Were these blacks slaves, as the two Spaniards said they were, and if they were slaves, to whom did they belong?

Captain Green, of Sag Harbor, made his way to New London too, for he wanted to claim, at the very least, the trunkful of doubloons that had been so close within his grasp.

Don José and Don Pedro wanted their property restored to them. But if Singbe and the others had committed murder on the high seas, they must be tried for piracy, and they could not be restored to their owners.

These were the knotty questions that faced Judge Judson on the morning of August 29, 1839, when he stepped aboard the *Washington* to open his court of inquiry.

5/The Inquiry

A large crowd assembled at the docks of the port of New London, but only a few would be allowed on board the *Washington* while the court of inquiry was held. The commander of the United States cutter *Experiment* volunteered to carry authorized persons out to the *Washington,* and his offer was received kindly by Judge Judson. So the party assembled — the judge, the court officials and clerks, the United States District Attorney's representative, C.A. Ingersoll, and a handful of newspapermen.

The issue was extremely complex, but the United States courts had precedents. One important case had occurred in the autumn of 1797, when the crew of H.M.S. *Hermione* mutinied on the high seas. The mutineers murdered the captain and his officers and ran the vessel into American waters, where they sold it and then scattered around the countryside.

Britain's officials were determined that these mutineers not go unpunished, and a worldwide investigation was begun by His Majesty's navy. A few months later the British consul at Charleston, South Carolina, came to the American authorities and insisted that they arrest a man who called himself Jonathan Robbins. This man, said the consul, was none other than Thomas Nash, ringleader of the mutineers.

After investigating, Judge Bee, of the United States District Court, wrote directly to President John Adams, because this was a problem in which both the judiciary and executive branches of the young republic were concerned. The judge wanted to know what the President thought ought to be done.

President Adams replied that under the treaty with Great Britain signed in 1795 the judge must hear the evidence against the man and decide whether there were grounds for yielding him to the British consul. If so, the British consul would summon a British naval vessel and take him to a British possession for trial on charges of mutiny and murder.

Judge Bee heard the evidence. A great furor arose in the United States. Robbins-Nash claimed that he was not a British citizen, but an American. He argued that he had been aboard the *Hermione* and had participated in the mutiny, but that he was an American citizen who had been seized and impressed by the British on the high seas. He had been taken from an American ship on the false statement of the British search-and-seizure party that he was an Irishman. He said that he was little better than a slave aboard the British vessel, that he had been illegally deprived of his freedom by the British, and that British admiralty law thus had no claim on him. He had a right, he asserted, to regain his liberty, no matter what he did to free himself.

But after listening to the evidence presented by the British consul and the British naval authorities, Judge Bee decided that Nash was the British sailor Robbins and that he should be returned to British jurisdiction. Robbins was taken aboard a British man-of-war, delivered to a British naval court which sat at Jamaica, convicted, and hanged for mutiny.

The issue of Jonathan Robbins then became a serious political matter in the United States. President Adams' enemies, members of the Democratic Republican party, maintained that he had acted improperly in delivering the sailor to the British.

Albert Gallatin, Democratic Republican leader in the House

of Representatives, rose to condemn President Adams. He said that as an impressed American, Robbins-Nash had every right to do what he did.

John Marshall, of Virginia, rose in defense of the Federalist President. The point was, said Marshall, that the case came within the limitations of the United States-British treaty of 1795. Whether or not the prisoner should have been delivered to the British was a matter of the facts, not a matter of judicial consideration.

What relationship did this bear to the *Amistad* case? Congressman Marshall had indicated that the evidence in the Robbins-Nash case showed that Robbins-Nash was *not* an American, but a British subject. But had Robbins-Nash been an American, Marshall said, neither he nor any other member of Congress would take the position that Robbins-Nash had been guilty of mutiny and murder. An impressed American seaman most certainly could commit homicide or take any other action he felt necessary to release himself from illegal deprivation of his liberty.

By extension, then, the question of the *Amistad's* slave crew was at issue.

On the day the judicial investigation was held in New London, few Americans were aware of the facts of the *Amistad* case. It was well known that a long, low, black schooner had been lurking off the Atlantic coast for several weeks and that it was believed to have been either a pirate ship or a ship manned by cannibals. It was also known that a schooner carrying slaves from Havana had been seized by the slaves.

Those who came to New London that late August day were interested in the sensation of the capture of the Negroes, and those who came aboard the *Washington* to conduct the court of inquiry were interested in justice, or in personal aggrandizement. They were not then thinking of the Robbins-Nash affair; but although the issue of British impressment of American sailors, which had kept the United States aroused for twenty years, had been ended with the War of 1812, and although that war was ancient history to the younger generation of 1839, the Robbins-Nash affair was not forgotten in the United States, and the matter of slave mutinies was very much alive.

Aboard the *Washington,* the court assembled in the captain's cabin. The marshal opened the hearing.

First Don Pedro Montes and Don José Ruiz were sworn. They filed a complaint that Joseph Cinquez (Singbe) had led thirty-eight other slaves (whose Spanish names were set down in the complaint just as they had been taken from the document prepared in Havana), and that these slaves had committed murder and piracy aboard the Spanish schooner *Amistad.*

Once the complaint was in writing and framed as an indictment, Singbe was brought in, manacled. He stood to hear the indictment he could not understand. He was wearing white duck sailor's trousers and a red flannel shirt. Around his neck was a cord, and suspended from it was a snuff box. He was an imposing and brave figure who impressed the spectators and the court, although they recoiled from the crime he was accused of having committed.

The presentation of evidence began. Lieutenant Commander Gedney and Lieutenant Meade presented several bundles of letters they had taken from the cabin of the *Amistad.* These were opened and read and were discovered to be Captain Ferrer's past business correspondence. They were put aside, except for two pertinent papers. These were the licenses issued by Governor General Ezpeleta of Cuba. One authorized Don Pedro Montes to transport three slaves to Principe. The other authorized Señor Don José Ruiz to transport forty-nine slaves to Principe, and then to report the arrival of these slaves to the territorial judge.

Don José Ruiz indicated the value of his cargo, in addition to the slaves, cargo that had been lost through wanton destruction or consumed by the slaves in the course of their journey. There were 10 dozen glass knobs, 39,500 needles, 48 rolls of

wire, 45 bottles of essence — the liquor that made the Negroes
so sick and drunk — 25 boxes of raisins, 500 pounds of jerked
beef, 25 bags of Spanish beans, and 50 pairs of shirts and pantaloons.

Don Pedro produced a license that authorized him to travel
to Matanzas for trading purposes, for he was a merchant. Don
José simply produced a passport, which showed that he was a
planter and the son of a planter.

Other basic proofs were introduced: the seaman's licenses belonging to the two Spanish sailors who had fled the ship the
night of the killings, the slave's license that had allowed the dead
Celestino to become a member of the crew and travel in Spanish
waters, and the papers of the dead captain.

Lieutenant Meade testified that he had boarded the *Amistad*
in behalf of the United States government. He had been met
immediately by Señor Ruiz, he said, and on his demand for
the papers, the Spaniard had first asked the protection of the
United States government and when that was assured, had found
them and handed them over.

Señor Ruiz was then sworn and became an official witness.
His testimony was translated for the court by Lieutenant Meade,
who spoke fluent Spanish.

"I brought 49 slaves in Havana," he said, "and shipped them
on board the schooner *Amistad*. We sailed for Guanaja, the
intermediate port for Principe. For the four first days every
thing went on well. In the night I heard a noise in the forecastle. All of us were asleep except the man at the helm. I
do not know how things began; I was awakened by the noise."

First, Don José said, he saw Singbe (whom he called Joseph)
when he led the others to attack the whites. It was dark because
there was no moon, and the darkness made the attack more
frightening and more effective than it would otherwise have
been. He could not tell how many of the slaves were engaged
in the attack.

"I took up an oar," he continued, "and tried to quell the

mutiny. I cried 'No! No!' Then I heard one of the crew cry, 'Murder!'"

"I then heard the captain order the cabin boy to go below and get some bread to throw to them in hope to pacify the Negroes. I went below and called on Montes to follow me and told them not to kill me; I did not see the captain killed."

He described how he had gone below and how he had been unharmed.

"They called me on deck" he continued, "and told me I should not be hurt. I asked them as a favor to spare the old man [Don Pedro Montes]. They did so."

"After this they went below and ransacked the trunks of the passengers. Before doing this they tied our hands. We went on our course — I don't know who was at the helm."

Only the next day had Don José discovered more or less what had happened on the night of the mutiny. He missed the captain. He missed the two sailors, Manuel and Yacinto, and Celestino the cook.

The following day the slaves indicated that they had killed all the others, but Antonio, the cabin boy, privately told Don José the truth — that the two sailors had escaped in the ship's after boat.

In some detail Don José described the manner in which the two white men had attempted to foil the efforts of their captors to sail back to Africa.

"We were compelled to steer east in the day; but sometimes the wind would not allow us to steer east; then they would threaten us with death. In the night we steered west and kept to the northward as much as possible."

And that was how they managed to make their way from Cuban waters to the waters of Long Island Sound, Don José explained.

The mutineers were a bloodthirsty lot, he indicated. They threatened the men constantly and they would have killed Antonio — even though he was a black African himself with only a dozen years of residence in Cuba — but he was their one link with the unfriendly outside world of the Americas.

When Don José had finished his testimony, the judge heard Don Pedro Montes, the old man whose life had truly been in jeopardy every moment during the trip. His story was basically the same as that of Don José.

He remembered that it was very dark on the night of the mutiny, and that he had finally lain down to sleep about midnight. It was later, sometime between three and four o'clock in the morning, that he had heard the sounds of a scuffle and discovered that Celestino, the cook, was being murdered. He armed himself with a stick and a knife, hoping to protect himself, but these gestures were apparently misunderstood by Singbe, who was wielding his deadly cane knife. Singbe wounded him twice, once on the head and once on the arm, before Don Pedro could escape and run below where he hid between two barrels, wrapped in a sail.

During his testimony, Don Pedro became very emotional, recalling how closely death had brushed him, and he called for his snuff box, to take a refreshing pinch. Then he went on.

"The prisoner rushed after me and attempted to kill me but was prevented by the interference of another man," Don Pedro said. He remembered that Singbe struck him, but he was so dazed at the time that he could not recall the face or name of the slave who saved his life. He had not only been dazed, he said, he was also faint from loss of blood from the head wound.

After Singbe was persuaded not to kill Don Pedro, he ordered both white men on deck to be tied together, and then Don Pedro was told to take the wheel and steer for Africa.

At first he was so afraid that he did as he was told. But on the second day after the mutiny heavy weather set in, and the Negroes were either sick or too much concerned with keeping their feet in the gale to worry about direction. Don Pedro then began to inch back toward Havana.

"When recovered," he testified, "I steered for Havana in the night by the stars, but by the sun in the day, taking care to make no more way than possible."

After sailing 150 miles they came across an American merchant ship, but as the Negroes did not want to approach her, they did not hail. They met another ship and avoided her, too.

Don Pedro was asked what he knew of the murder of the captain. He said he knew nothing. As for the death of the mulatto, "All I know of the murder of the mulatto, is that I heard the blows. He was asleep when attacked."

The next morning, Don Pedro continued, the Negroes washed down the decks, apparently to get rid of the blood. And, he added, every one of the Negroes seemed glad that the murders had been committed.

He lived in constant fear from that moment of capture on, Don Pedro declared. "The prisoners treated me harshly, and, but for the interference of others, would have killed me several times every day. We kept no reckoning, I did not know how many days we had been out, nor what day of the week it was when the officers came on board. We anchored at least thirty times and lost an anchor at New Providence [where they had landed for water]. When at anchor we were treated well, but at sea they acted cruelly toward me. They once wanted to drop anchor in the high seas. I had no wish to kill any of them, but prevented them from killing each other."

With that Don Pedro concluded his emotional testimony, and Judge Judson pondered for a moment. Then he ordered Singbe sent below to his cell, so the investigation could be continued.

The next move was to travel by ship's boat to the *Amistad,* to examine the scene of the crimes, and to take the testimony of Antonio, who was still aboard the schooner.

Antonio was called, the black Antonio who had for so many weeks trod so narrow a line, trying to propitiate the African savages who looked upon him as a white man's dog and who would have killed him gladly had they not needed his services as translator with the two Spaniards and for negotiations with the ships they encountered.

Antonio was addressed in Spanish by Lieutenant Meade. The first question was to determine whether or not he knew the nature of truth and an oath. He said that he knew quite well, he was a Christian.

He was sworn in the Christian manner, and began to tell about his experiences on the *Amistad*. He contributed significant details: "That night it had been raining very hard, and all hands had been on deck. [This situation accounted for the ease with which the slaves were able to surprise their unwary captors.]

"The rain ceased, but it was still very dark. Clouds covered the moon. After the rain the captain and the mulatto lay down on some mattresses they had brought on deck."

Antonio described how four slaves had crept up on the captain and the mulatto and had attacked them. "They struck the captain across the face two or three times; they struck the mulatto oftener. Neither of them groaned."

By the time the captain and the mulatto were dead the rest of the slaves had come on deck, all armed with the long, murderous cane knives.

While this was going on, Antonio saw the two Spanish crewmen escape in the boat. He was awake during the entire attack and saw everything that happened. He confirmed Montes' story of capture: "After killing the captain and the cook and wounding Señor Montes, they tied Montes and Ruiz by the hands till they had ransacked the cabin. After doing so they loosed them, and they went below. Señor Montes could scarcely walk."

Most important, Antonio identified the four slaves who had killed the captain and the mulatto: Singbe and three others (one of whom had since died). He went below decks and picked out the other two accomplices: Grabo and Konoma, the man from the Congo with sharply filed teeth.

One tour around the decks of the *Amistad* and the judge and investigators had enough of the evil-smelling schooner and disembarked to reconvene in the captain's cabin of the *Washington*. All that remained to be done was for Judge Judson to reach a decision.

Had it been mutiny?

Were these slaves guilty of murder — or, to put it more judicially, was there enough evidence that they had committed murder to go to trial?

Everyone aboard the *Washington* that day was convinced that this was an obvious case of murder and piracy on the high seas. The evidence was overwhelming.

The judge handed down his decision then and there: "Joseph Cinquez, the leader, and 38 others, as named in the indictment, stand committed for trial before the next Circuit Court at Hartford to be holden on the 17th day of September next.

"The three girls and Antonio the cabin boy are ordered to give bonds in the sum of $100 each to appear before the said court and give evidence in the aforesaid case."

Since the little girls and Antonio did not have $100 among them, all were also committed to jail for safekeeping.

Then the witnesses were ordered to give $100 bonds that they would appear in court. They were Lieutenant Meade, Don José, and Don Pedro. The United States marshal was given an order by the court to transport the prisoners and witnesses to the jail at New Haven, and the inquiry was ended.[2]

6/Storm Center

Don José Ruiz and Don Pedro Montes were Spanish gentlemen to the last drop of blood, a fact indicated in an advertisement they placed that very day, August 29, in the newspapers of New London.[1]

A Card

The subscribers, Don José Ruiz and Don Pedro Montes, in gratitude for their most unhoped for and most providential rescue from the hands of a ruthless gang of African buccaneers, and an awful death, would take this means of expressing, in some slight degree, their thankfulness and obligations to Lieutenant Commander T.R. Gedney, and the officers and crew of the U.S. surveying brig *Washington*, for their decision in seizing the *Amistad*, and their unremitting kindness and hospitality in providing for their comfort on board their vessel, as well as the means they have taken for the protection of their property.

We also must express our indebtedness to that nation whose flag they so worthily bear, with an assurance that this act will be duly appreciated by our most gracious sovereign, Her Majesty the Queen of Spain.

Don José Ruiz
Don José Montes

But gracious as the card appeared to be, there was more than grace to it: the advertisement was a signal to the world that the Spaniards considered the Africans to be their property and expected to have them restored to their possession. It was also a signal to those rescuers, Lieutenant Commander Gedney and Lieutenant Meade, that they would not be able to claim the *Amistad* and its cargoes, goods and human, without a struggle with the Spanish, who were secure in their belief that they would be backed to the hilt by their government.

And why should they not be backed?

Slaves were slaves. The United States government recognized a man's property right in slaves, and Congress, although urged hundreds of times by the growing army of abolitionists, had flatly refused to interfere with the institution of slavery in the Southern states. Congress would not even legislate to abolish the slave markets or slavery in Washington, the national capital.

Indeed, slavery could not even be debated openly in Congress, at least in the House of Representatives. In May, 1836, Congress was deluged with petitions by various abolitionist and religious groups concerning slavery. In order to control the petitions three resolutions were offered in the House of Representatives that month: one said that Congress had no constitutional right to interfere with slavery in the states; a second said that Congress ought not to interfere with slavery in the District of Columbia, which was directly governed by Congress; a third said that all propositions relative to slavery in the future should be laid on the table and no action at all should be taken on them. In other words, petitions relative to slavery could be offered Congress under the citizen's right to petition, but Congress had no responsibility to pay attention to the petitions.

The third resolution was challenged by Representative John Quincy Adams of Massachusetts, son of the John Adams who had been President at the time of the H.M.S. *Hermione* mutiny, and a former President himself. Adams had served a single term

as President, but he had served and was to serve many terms in
the House, and he was to become the most eloquent of Congressmen.

Representative Adams wished to object to the third resolution
as limiting or even effectively destroying the right of the public
to petition Congress. He arose, but was not recognized by the
Speaker, who instead recognized a representative from Georgia,
who moved to shut off debate. The House so voted, before
Adams or any other objectors had been heard.

"Am I gagged or am I not?" asked Adams.

Thus was named the famous Gag Resolution of 1836, and
if memory of the *Hermione* mutiny case was dimmed in America
in 1839, memory of the Gag Rule and the growing struggle
over slavery was bright as a silver penny.

Just the year before, the Whig movement had been badly
shaken in an argument over the annexation of the Republic
of Texas, and one of the essential points of the argument was
that it would be a slave state. Henry Clay, a Whig, had on
February 7, 1839, delivered a strong speech in which he attempted to convince the world and his party that there was no
reason to identify the Whigs with abolition. But in the North
such Whigs as the editors of the Hartford *Courant* gainsaid
his position: they were stalwart abolitionists, and John Quincy
Adams, known in the South as "The Madman of Massachusetts,"
was forever abrading the national unity by bringing up the
discussion of slavery and abolition.

In this autumn of 1839 Don José and Don Pedro had every
right to believe their property would be returned to them by
the courts.[2]

Lieutenant Commander Gedney and Lieutenant Meade had
a different view. They, too, respected the rights of property
in slaves as well as the inanimate cargo; but they claimed
that when the brig *Washington* came upon the *Amistad,* it was,
to all intents and purposes, a derelict, the captain murdered by
the slaves aboard, without crew and without hope of survival.

It was their initiative that had rescued the Spanish gentlemen, and the ship, goods, and the slaves should belong to the officers. If their position was to be accepted by the courts, they would become relatively wealthy men, for while Don José had paid $450 each for his 49 Negro slaves in Havana, the going price in the United States slave markets was $1,000 to $1,500 per head for such young and healthy slaves.

That August day, to carry out the orders of the court, the Africans were put aboard a small sloop under the command of Lieutenant Holcomb of the *Washington* — all except Singbe, the ringleader of the mutiny, who was adjudged to be dangerous. He was separated from the other Negroes, manacled, and sent ahead on another small sloop, under the charge of Captain Mather Herald, who had been hired by United States Marshal Wilcox to see Singbe safely in the New Haven jail. The others came along at a more leisurely pace, arriving after Singbe, in the charge of Holcomb and Colonel Pendleton, keeper of the New Haven jail. They were not manacled, not being considered dangerous.

The two Spanish gentlemen went to Boston to lay out their case for return of their property and to consult with Her Majesty's officials at the consulate there. Lieutenant Commander Gedney and Lieutenant Meade consulted with lawyers to prepare their case for the granting of salvage rights on ship and cargo to them.

So the *Amistad* created work for a number of lawyers. And there has seldom been a ship's arrival that aroused more interest in the towns and villages of the northeastern United States. The *Amistad* had been well advertised up and down the coast by the many reports of sighting of the "pirate" vessel. Her capture had been detailed in the newspapers, and particularly in the important New York *Sun,* which had devoted nearly a full page to the story — a space usually reserved for wars, catastrophes, and political campaigns.

Singbe arrived first, accompanied by the revenue cutter *Wolcott* and Captain Herald. The cutter put into shore at New

Haven's Long Wharf, and Captain Mather escorted his prisoner
on foot up Chapel Street to the New Haven Green, past the
Tontine House where the gentry stayed, and around the back
of the County House, where they walked through the tavern
kept by Colonel Pendleton, and thus into the jail.

Singbe, of course, was the center of the tavern's attraction
as he marched through the smokey air, and was characterized
as "one of the cannibals" from the *Amistad*. He was kept over-
night with the common prisoners.

The next day when the word came that the rest of the "cannibals" would be arriving at Long Wharf, half of New Haven
turned out to see them. The prisoners came in a strange, ragged
procession, Konoma leading those strong enough to march, with
the four children scampering about, and two wagons loaded with
those too weak to walk to jail. All were guarded by armed
sailors from the *Washington*, who had been detailed to the
sloop.

In the combination tavern-jail, Colonel Pendleton put the
sick on the third floor and the others into cells on the second
floor. The four children were taken by Mrs. Pendleton to a
private room in the rear of the tavern.

It was Sunday, and after church and Sunday dinner more
of the townspeople came to the green to gawk at the captives.
It was the most exciting show in town. Colonel Pendleton was
a hard-headed businessman, and he quickly established a fee
of a shilling (25¢), with the promise that the money would go
for the betterment of the Africans after the expenses of their
incarceration were met.

Dr. Charles Hooker, professor of medicine at Yale college and
a well-known local physician, was asked to examine the sick
captives. Most of these complained of bowel disorders, the result of eating unfamiliar food, too little food, and a totally un-
balanced diet for three months.

Professor Josiah Willard Gibbs of the college also came to see
the captives. He was Yale's senior professor of Semitic languages,

Latin, and Greek, and a world-famous figure in the study of the tongues of the ancients. He brought with him several works dealing with the tongues of Africa, hoping to be able to place these natives and then to find an interpreter for them.

Various entrepreneurs came to see the captives, too, hoping to be able to capitalize on their sudden fame. Phrenologists came to measure their skulls and to discourse learnedly about their characteristics. A Mr. Fletcher, for example, examined Singbe's skull bumps and gave the following analysis:

> Cingque appears to be about 26 years of age, powerful frame, bilious and sanguine temperament, bilious predominating. His head by measurement is 22⅝ inches in circumference, 15 inches from the root of the nose to the occipital protuberance over the top of the head, 15 inches from the Meatus Auditorius to do, over the head, and 5¾ inches through the head at destructiveness.
>
> The development of the faculties is as follows:
>
> Firmness; self-esteem; hope — very large.
>
> Benevolence; veneration; conscientiousness; approbativeness; wonder; concentrativeness; inhabitiveness; comparison; form — large. Amativeness; philoprogenitiveness; adhesiveness; combativeness; destructiveness; secretiveness, constructiveness; caution; language; individuality; eventuality; causality; order — average. Alimentiveness; acquisitiveness; ideality; mirthfulness; imitation; size; weight; color; locality; number; time; tune — moderate and small. The head is well-formed and such as a phrenologist admires. The coronal region being the largest, the frontal and occipital nearly balanced, and the basilar moderate. In fact, such an African head is seldom to be seen, and doubtless in other circumstances would have been an honor to his race.[3]

The phrenologist's report was an indication of a new emotion that had begun to assert itself in relation to the African captives, even within twenty-four hours of their arrival. The emotion was sympathy.

Although the villagers and townspeople of the New Haven

area came to the jail to gape at "cannibals," others in the New England community quickly disabused themselves and their friends of the idea that these were man-eating savages bent on the destruction of the white race.

Within three days after the arrival of the captives at the jail, abolitionists in New York City had moved to help the unfortunate Africans who spoke no English and who had obviously come to the shores of the United States so unwillingly.[4] The Reverend Joshua Leavitt, one of the city's leading antislavery men, was chosen to go to New Haven and examine the unfortunates.

He made the voyage by water, the most expeditious manner, and wrote his report, published in the New York *Commercial Advertiser*.[5]

On his arrival in New Haven, Mr. Leavitt went to the jail, where he found the Africans "occupying four of five apartments" under the care of United States Marshal Wilcox. He found them comfortable, or as comfortable as possible considering their confinement.

Marshal Wilcox was not in attendance the day Mr. Leavitt called, for the marshal had been called to New London to make an inventory of the slave ship and its contents. Lieutenant Commander Gedney and Lieutenant Meade had indeed filed their suit for salvage rights, and one of the first legal steps was to discover exactly what was under consideration. Mr. Leavitt spoke to jailer Pendleton, but the assistant did not have the right to take the prisoners onto the green for exercise under guard, and nothing could be done until Mr. Wilcox returned.

Otherwise Mr. Leavitt did not see much cause for concern about the prisoners' physical treatment. Most of them had been decently clothed, by American standards, before they left the *Amistad*. They were wearing cotton shirts and trousers. Arrangements had been made for them to have woolen shirts and trousers when the weather became inclement.

Mr. Leavitt had brought with him an old African who could speak the languages of the Congo. But when the old man began to talk, none of the Africans could understand more than a few words. Disappointed, Mr. Leavitt vowed to continue his efforts to find an interpreter.

He saw Singbe, and remarked that he bore a good resemblance to the prints that were being sold about the streets of every city in the land. Artist James Sheffield, who had made the drawings aboard the *Washington* for the New London *Gazette*, had sold the rights far and near.

Sympathy was growing for these people, and one reason was that no one seemed able to understand their language. Even Singbe seemed gentle to Mr. Leavitt, although he was obviously contemplating his coming execution without joy and was far more depressed than any of the others. "They all appear to be persons of quiet minds and a mild and cheerful temper," said Mr. Leavitt. "There are no contentions among them; even the poor children, three girls and one boy, who are in a room by themselves, seem to be uniformly kind and friendly."[6]

The matter of court action was not yet settled in these first days of September, and it was a serious problem. Obviously, if the slaves were property they could not be tried for the human crimes of murder and piracy.

What was to be done?

Newspapers in New England and the Middle States speculated on the course of events. The Africans were "committed to trial" at the next circuit court, but trial for what crimes?

The Hartford *Courant* stated the puzzling questions a week after the Negroes had been brought to New Haven.[7] The public was instructed in the fine points of piracy and salvage, as interpreted in the year 1839 in the United States.

Ward's *Laws of Nations* was quoted to establish the fact that piracy, once considered honorable work, was regarded by Western Society as one of the most serious of crimes (Ward

I. 177). The writer Azuni, an expert on maritime law, was quoted to establish the definition of a pirate: ". . . one who roves the sea in an armed vessel, without any commission or passport from any prince or sovereign state, but solely on his own authority, and for the purpose of seizing by force, and appropriating to himself, indiscriminately, every vessel he may meet. . . " (Azuni's *Maritime Law*, Vol 2. 351)

Other learned quotations from the law were brought forth to elucidate the issue. The case of United States v. Smith (Wheaton Reports 153) showed that one court held: "Robbery or forcible depradations upon the sea, *animo furandi* (with the intent of theft) is piracy by the law of nations and by the act of Congress."

Kent's *Commentaries* I. 171 defined piracy as robbery on the high seas.

Congress on April 30, 1790, had passed a law which, in Section 8, declared that murder or robbery on the high seas or in any place out of the jurisdiction of the particular states should be called piracy, as should any other offense punishable by death if committed in the United States. It said further that if any seaman should mutiny, he too should be called a pirate. This body of law was affirmed again on May 15, 1820, when Congress said that anyone who committed robbery on the high seas or any place where the sea ebbed or flowed, should be adjudged a pirate.

The *Courant's* position, however, was that the Africans could not possibly be considered pirates. "Under the definition of piracy given by the law of nations the prisoners are certainly not pirates," said the *Courant's* legal authority. They did not "rove the sea" for the purpose of seizing other vessels. On the contrary, "they were on board the *Amistad* by compulsion."

The legal expert went further: "If by the law of nations they are not pirates, are they made so by the acts of Congress mentioned above?" Here he was specifically raising the question of the deaths of Captain Ferrer and the mulatto cook. Certainly the *Amistad* captives were not pirates by this definition, either, "unless they have committed the crime of murder or robbery."

The *Courant* writer went on: "Murder is killing with malice aforethought. The slaves on board the *Amistad* did not kill with *malice* aforethought, but they took the lives of their captors to regain their own liberty."

Here he made a telling point: "They had been recently stolen from the coast of Africa and if they had been kidnaped by an American citizen, this act itself would have been piracy." He was referring to the Act of Congress of May 15, 1820, which reaffirmed the United States enmity toward the international slave trade.

"That they had a right by force to regain their liberty cannot be doubted, and if in the act they killed their keepers, they were not guilty of murder."

The *Courant* writer also said it seemed impossible to believe they were guilty of robbery, and he quoted East's *Crown Law,* Vol 2. 707, to prove it: "Robbery is a felonious taking of money or goods of any value from the person of another, or in his presence, against his will, by violence or putting him in fear."

Did the *Amistad* captives commit robbery?

"Now although it is said that the Negroes took some of the goods and money, yet they did not do this by violence and putting the owners in fear. They did indeed put the owners in fear, but not by taking or in the act of taking their property, nor had their violence or the terror they inspired anything to do with the taking of the goods or money."

No, said the writer, the *Amistad* captives had not committed robbery. They did not know the value of what they took, and it was not to secure any objects of value that they had risen against the captain and crew.

"If, then," continued the *Courant's* advocate, "they were not guilty of murder or robbery, they are not pirates by the acts of Congress, unless their 'revolt' was such a one as is intended by the statute. But the revolt there spoken of must be made by a 'seaman.' These Negroes were certainly not seamen, and they of course cannot be included in the act relating to revolts by seamen."

As is sometimes the case with advocates, the *Courant* then adjusted the facts of the case slightly in order to strengthen the opinion. Where some of the Africans at least (as would become known later) were quite familiar with firearms because they had used them for hunting in Africa, the *Courant,* in telling the story of the capture, indicated that none of them knew anything about the use of firearms, and so had left the four muskets. In fact, the Negroes had not left the muskets alone, but had fired them at ships. However, the *Courant's* editors were doing their best to make a case for black innocence corrupted by white evil.

In the matter of Lieutenant Commander Gedney's claims to salvage, the *Courant's* authority was more sympathetic. Salvage, he explained, was demandable for vessels saved from pirates or the enemy, and he quoted Chancellor Kent (3 *Commentaries* 197) to prove it. The naval officers could expect perhaps half or a quarter of the value of the ship and cargo.

The *Courant* also raised the question of where the *Amistad* captives and the salvage case might be tried, and agreed that the Federal District Court was the proper place.

Preparations were continuing to bring the Negroes before the District Court, but a serious problem developed: How could they be tried when they could not understand the proceedings and no one could understand them?

This matter demanded the immediate attention of the court and the community. Professor Gibbs, the expert on linguistics, addressed himself to the problem. As he had no basis for understanding the Africans, he must create one. Visiting them in their jail cell, he became aware that the predominant language among them was one called Mendi, and he began scouring the New Haven waterfront for an African sailor who could speak this language. He was unsuccessful.

Professor Gibbs returned to the Africans. He held up a single finger and said, "One."

"Eta," replied one of the Africans.

And so the counting began.

"Eta."

"Fili."

"Kiauwa."

"Naeni."

"Loelu."

He learned to count to ten in this language, memorized the sounds, and wrote down the transliteration in English characters to stimulate his memory.

With so meager a weapon, Professor Gibbs then set out for the larger waterfront of New York City, to search the wharves and shipping companies for a man familiar with the Mandingo country of Africa; he was now certain that this was the region from which the *Amistad* captives came.

In New York, people were concerned with the plight of the *Amistad* captives on an entirely different level. The Reverend Joshua Leavitt had returned from New Haven with a positive and favorable report on what he had seen and the problem that the Negroes and the nation faced. Abolitionists in the city were quick to act and to raise a committee for the defense of the captives.

Three men came forth to form this committee. Mr. Leavitt was one of them. Another was the Reverend Simeon S. Jocelyn, who had for some time served as pastor of a Negro church in New Haven. The third was Lewis Tappan, a merchant of Hanover Square, New York, who was totally committed to the cause of the abolition of slavery. He and his brother Arthur were two of the major props of the New York chapter of the American Anti-Slavery Society.

The principal office for the informal committee was that of *The Emancipator,* the publication of the Anti-Slavery Society, which Mr. Leavitt edited.

In the pages of *The Emancipator* the committee announced

its formation and solicited donations for the support and legal
aid of the Africans. They appealed for money and clothing and
began to work to find legal counsel for the Africans. They obtained the services of Seth P. Staples and Theodore Sedgwick
of New York, and of Roger S. Baldwin of New Haven.[8] Lewis
Tappan went to New Haven, taking with him three Africans
whom he hoped might be able to speak with the *Amistad* captives in their own tongues.

They arrived in New Haven on the evening of September
6. A day later, two more Africans joined them, sent by the others
of the Committee on Behalf of the African Prisoners, as it called
itself.[9]

The next morning the committeemen went to the jail to try
to communicate with Singbe and his companions. One of the
three Africans, it turned out, could carry on rudimentary con-
versations with some of the captives. He was from the country of
the Gissi, about a hundred miles inland from the Gallinas River,
well inland from the Mendi country, but still close enough for
him to have had contact with the Mendis and learned some
words of their language. He knew more of the language of the
Gallinas area, because he, too, had been enslaved and held for
months in the *barracoons* of Lomboko, before being transported to Colombia. There he was liberated in the uprising led
by Simon Bolivar against the Spanish.

The prisoners had been given striped prison garb, shirts and
trousers, for which they had exchanged their bits of finery and
oddments of clothing. The girls had been given calico dresses
and shawls, but they had made turbans of the shawls as more
in keeping with their custom.

Tappan and his Africans found them in good humor, the more
so when the captives discovered at last a man who could speak
to them in language akin to their own tongue. "You may imagine
the joy manifested by these poor Africans," he wrote, "when they
heard one of their own color address them in a friendly manner,
and in a language they could comprehend!"

By the time Tappan arrived, the Negroes had learned some-

thing about the use of dishes and had stopped throwing their
tin plates on the floor as they did at first, being accustomed to
eating from plaintain skins or forest leaves and then discarding
them. They were well behaved and quiet. On the day before
Tappan's arrival the sheriff had taken them out for a ride in a
wagon, for there was little fear of most of the Africans at this
point.

Several of the *Amistad* captives were still sick. One had died
of dysentery early in the week and was buried ceremoniously
by the abolitionists.

When the African, who was named John Ferry, began to talk
to the prisoners, he discovered that as suspected nearly all of
them were from the Mendi or Mandingo country. Then the
visitors were taken by Colonel Pendleton, the jailer, to see
Singbe.

"He is with several savage-looking fellows, black and white,
who are in jail on various charges," Tappan wrote, with no apparent sense of irony. "Visitors are not allowed to enter this
stronghold of the jail, and the inmates can only be seen and conversed with through the aperture of the door."

But for the benefit of these visitors Colonel Pendleton brought
Singbe out. He was clad only in a blanket. At first he was
suspicious, because he had been called out time and again for
the inspection of various white curiousity-seekers. But when
John Ferry talked to him in a language he understood, Singbe
softened, and the whites began to learn something about him
and his life. Tappan wrote:

> Towards evening, we made a visit to Shidquau [Singbe] and
> conversed with him a considerable time. He drew his hand across
> his throat, as his room mates said he had done frequently before,
> and asked whether the people here intended to kill him.
>
> He was assured that probably no harm would happen to him —
> that we were his friends — and that he would be sent across the
> ocean towards the rising sun, home to his friends.
>
> His countenance immediately lost the anxious and distressed

expression it had before, and beamed with joy. He says he was born about two days travelling from the ocean; that he purchased some goods, and being able to pay for only two-thirds of the amount, he was seized by the traders, his own countrymen, and sold to King Sharka for the remaining third.

Singbe added other details of his life. He told the whites about his father and his wife and his three children, one of them about as old as the little African girls who were prisoners, and two others older.

Tappan was very much interested in Singbe's religion: "We endeavored to ascertain what his ideas were about a Supreme Being, if he had any. He said 'God is good.'" He did not go into theology further.

They asked Singbe then about education and reading and writing, and he told them that none of his countrymen could read or write.

On Saturday, September 7, while seeing the prisoners during the day, Lewis Tappan was also busy with the lawyers. Lawyer Staples had come to New Haven from New York to consult with Roger Baldwin, who would be the chief of counsel. Tappan made arrangements with Colonel Pendleton for Singbe to be taken out of his cell for a period on Sunday, so that the two lawyers might examine him through interpreter Ferry.

The story that the captives began to unfold through even these halting interpretations gave the abolitionists material with which to work, and by the middle of the following week the Hartford *Courant* had strengthened its conclusions about the case: "A case of no trifling importance," wrote the editors, and warned that the *Amistad* case was vital to all America.

By the laws of the United States, the African slave trade is declared to be piracy and the persons engaged in it are liable to be punished as pirates. It would be very extraordinary then if these men, who had been stolen from their own country, and brought away for the purpose of being reduced to a state of slavery, should be punished in the United States for using such means as they possessed to extricate themselves from the power and custody of men who gained that custody by the perpetration of a crime which by our laws would cost them their lives. It would be a singular case if both parties in the same transaction should be held guilty of a capital offense and suffer the same penalty of the law for their crimes.

The *Courant* did not believe that there was any ground for legal action at all. No offense had been committed against the laws of the United States within the District of Connecticut, nor did the *Courant* believe there had been any violation of any American law by the Negroes: "On the contrary, the offense against our laws, if any has occurred, would seem to have been committed by those who brought the Negroes from Africa. They were pirates by our laws, and liable to be punished as such, if fairly brought within our jurisdiction."

The truth was, the *Courant* said, that the Spaniards were the offenders in the case and really had no business in calling on the American courts for redress of any supposed wrongs.

The *Courant's* position was important; it reflected that of the abolitionists. But the Spaniards were of quite a different mind in this matter. They had visited the Spanish consul in Boston, and he had communicated with the Spanish minister. Don José and Don Pedro were making an effort to secure restoration of their property, including the slaves. The Spanish Minister, Señor Angel Calderon de la Barca, came to New York to see the two Spanish gentlemen and he prepared a letter to Secretary of State John Forsyth, which was sent on September 6.

The minister expressed proper gratitude for the salvation of his two countrymen by Lieutenant Commander Gedney: "That conduct will be appreciated as it deserves by my august sovereign, and by the Spanish Government, and will be reciprocated on similar occasions by the Spaniards — a people ever grateful for benefits received."[10]

But beneath the genteel exterior there was a note of annoyance.

"The act of humanity thus performed," the minister said, "would have been complete, had the vessel at the same time been set at liberty, and the Negroes sent to be tried by the proper tribunal, and by the violated laws of the country of which they are subjects. The undersigned is willing to believe that such would have been the case, had the General Government been able to interpose its authority in the first instance, as it has probably done during the short interval between the occurrence of this affair and the period when the undersigned received an authentic statement of the facts."[11]

The Spanish minister was not the only one who was annoyed. United States District Attorney W.S. Holabird, a loyal Democrat and no lover of slaves or abolitionists, was very much distressed by the entire proceedings. Had there been any way in which he could have done it, he would have sent the Spaniards and their slaves in the *Amistad* to Cuba or anywhere else out of his judicial district. He wrote the Secretary of State: "It appears from the evidence that the blacks were taken on board the schooner at a port in the island of Cuba, to transport to another port in the same island; when from seven to ten leagues out, they murdered the captain and mate, and took possession of the schooner...."

If the editors of the Hartford *Courant* had prejudged the case and said it was not murder, District Attorney Holabird had prejudged it too and decided it *was* murder. He was much distressed at having to face so unpleasant a political prospect as this offered: "The next term of our circuit court sits on the 17th instant, at which time I *suppose* it will be my duty to bring them to trial, unless they are in some other way disposed of. Should you have any instructions to give on the subject, I should like to receive them as soon as may be."

Holabird's letter, along with Don Angel's official letter, was immediately forwarded to that canny prince of politicians, President Martin Van Buren. The President did not wish to get involved in this issue at this time and he began to stall. First he asked, through Secretary Forsyth, for more information. That request was made on September 23, and by that time the legal questions of the *Amistad* captives were under consideration.

District Judge Judson had not been aware of the Spanish-American Treaty of Commerce and Amity of 1795 when he ordered the *Amistad* captives to stand trial. Early in September he was apprised of the treaty, in the following way:

Señor Antonio Vega, the Spanish consul at Boston, received a copy of Don Añgel's letter to the Secretary of State, with instructions to go to Connecticut and see if he could not expedite matters by persuading the court to turn the *Amistad* captives over to Don José and Don Pedro, along with the *Amistad* and everything aboard her, without payment for salvage. No American court was competent to adjudge this case, said the minister. The Negroes were to be conveyed somehow to Havana for trial. Also, if the authorities in Connecticut interfered, the two Spaniards should be indemnified for injury done to them.

Furthermore, the consul was prodded by the same words sent to the Secretary of State, citing the Spanish-American Treaty.[12] It was clear in the treaty — a case could be made that the treaty covered the situation. One article provided that if a Spanish vessel came into American waters for any "urgent necessity," it should be succored and allowed to return out of ports or roads or anywhere without hindrance.

It also stipulated that all ships and merchandise "of what nature soever" that were rescued from pirates or robbers should be restored entirely. The Spaniards claimed the slaves were merchandise. Another article said each country must give the same assistance to nationals of the other country as it would to its own nationals.

All these clauses could be held to indicate that the slaves must be returned to Don José and Don Pedro.

Consul Vega went to Winsted, Connecticut, to see District

Attorney Holabird, and presented his case there, just as it was being presented in Washington.

The district attorney became more and more disturbed. It was a case of being hanged if he did and hanged if he did not, as far as he could see. The *Amistad* affair threatened to blossom into a full-scale political scandal, and he wanted, if possible to throw it into the hands of the Secretary of State. Since the Secretary was a Georgian by birth, there was little question as to his views on the matter. Nor was there any question about Martin Van Buren's views: the *Amistad* affair threatened Democratic party unity, and he would have liked to have been relieved of it too.

District Attorney Holabird wrote to the Secretary of State on September 9 from Hartford. He had looked up the treaty, he had conferred with others, and he was still hopeful that the executive branch of the government would rush in to save him the trouble of trying so difficult and unrewarding a case.

He cited several legal references that referred to cases involving foreign vessels, piracy on the high seas, and foreign nationals. "I would respectfully inquire, sir," the district attorney said, "whether there are no treaty stipulations with the government of Spain that would authorize our Government to deliver them up to the Spanish authorities; and if so, whether it could be done before our court sits?"

Secretary of State Forsyth could answer quickly when he and the President wished. The Spanish minister did not have a reply to his note until September 16, but five days before that the District Attorney had his answer:

He was to bide his time.

"In the meantime," said the Secretary of State, "you will take care that no proceeding of your circuit court, or of any other judicial tribunal, places the vessel, cargo, or slaves beyond control of the Federal Executive."

When Holabird received that letter, it was apparent to him that he was being asked to do the impossible. If he took the

Amistad case into court (and there was nothing else he could do with it because the wheels had been started by Judge Judson), it would automatically put the vessel, cargo, and slaves beyond the control of the Federal Executive. The best the district attorney could hope for was a continuance, which would stall the case for a time.

In the climate pervading New England in September, 1839, it would have been extremely difficult for any man to stall the *Amistad* captives' case. Nearly every newspaper in the land had carried articles about the affair; advertisers were using pictures and the words, "the long, low, black schooner" to drag readers into consideration of their wares. Thus stalling was patently unwise politically, and probably impossible juridically. The only manner in which action could be taken was to declare the President's interest in the affair and indicate that he was considering the return of the *Amistad* captives to Spanish jurisdiction under the Treaty of 1795.

From everywhere in abolitionist country — Pennsylvania and Massachusetts, New York and Rhode Island, Maine and Ohio — came contributions for the defense of the *Amistad* captives. The newspapers printed the letters that accompanied the drafts when they were cogent and persuasive, as was one such letter from William Jay, of Bedford, to Lewis Tappan.[13]

Jay pointed out one of the anomalies of the Spanish case. On June 28, 1835, Spain and Great Britain had concluded a treaty supplementary to that of 1820 outlawing the slave trade. The new treaty declared that the slave trade on the part of Spain had been totally and finally abolished in all parts of the world. Two months after ratification, Spain promised to promulgate a penal law throughout the Spanish dominions, inflicting severe punishment on Spanish subjects who under any pretext took part in the slave trade. Every vessel in any way involved in the slave trade was to be broken up and sold piecemeal to prevent its ever again being so used.

Between January 1, 1829, and January 1, 1836, it will be

recalled, twenty-nine Spanish slavers had been condemned by
the Mixed Court at Havana, having been captured by cruisers
off Cuba and brought in to port. In November, 1838, the Queen
of Spain had ordered the Governor General of the island to
wipe out the slave trade. The Governor General, of course,
was one of the worst offenders in the islands and took a personal head tax on every slave brought in or taken out.

But if the practice was evil, the intent of the Spanish crown
was clear and the law was in effect. The international trade in
slaves was illegal, and the *Amistad* slaves could not be considered to be slaves under the Spanish law. Don José and Don
Pedro had committed crimes against the Spanish government
and should be liable for trial in Spanish courts.

But would they be tried? And would the *Amistad* captives
be freed if they were sent back to Havana?

The abolitionists said no, they would not. The Spanish minister
had already indicated his government's prejudgment of the
case, and the abolitionists were not willing to see the captives
delivered into the unfriendly hands of the Spanish.

On September 14 the *Amistad* captives were taken from the
New Haven jail and moved to Hartford by canal boat to await
their trial. There were fewer of them now: two had died of
dysentery since they had been in jail. Another, Burna, the Mendi
blacksmith, was confined to his bed in New Haven, too ill to
make the trip, and he was excused. Singbe, accorded special
treatment, was brought up alone.

Two days later a reporter from the Hartford *Courant* called
on the *Amistad* captives in the Hartford jail. Singbe had arrived
a day later than the others, but he, too, was there, and was
now allowed to remain with his fellows.

Half a dozen of the *Amistad* captives were still sick with
dysentery, but they were improving daily, and all of them were
putting on weight. The children, and some of the others were
beginning to learn English, under the tutelage of some of their
abolitionist friends. Antonio was still with them, but he was con-

fined to one corner of the room and was given a wide berth by all the others. Their dislike showed very plainly even to a reporter who had never seen them before and did not speak their language.

The *Courant* spoke for Hartford when it said, after its reporter had visited the captives: "Whatever may be the fate of these poor Africans, a strong feeling of sympathy is manifested in their behalf, and we presume the wish that they may be permitted to return to their country and their homes is universal in this community."[14]

Throughout New England, except of course among those who defended slavery, the attitude was very much the same.

7/The Trial of the Captives I

United States District Attorney Holabird was pleased in one respect with the results of his correspondence with Secretary of State Forsyth: it had taken the responsibility off his back, and no matter what happened in the trial he would not be held personally accountable for the fate of the captives of the *Amistad*. He was so pleased with himself that he showed the letter from Forsyth to a friend, and the friend told another friend, and soon the secret was out — before the trial — and Roger Sherman Baldwin, chief of counsel for the *Amistad* captives, had an indication of the government's case that he might not otherwise have been granted.

Baldwin's answer was to prepare a writ of habeas corpus, for presentation either to the Circuit Court or the District Court, as matters sorted themselves out. The Circuit Court would rule on the jurisdictional questions involved, and then if there was to be a trial on specific charges the District Court would try the case.

The abolitionists had made plans, too, if the case should go against the captives, to spirit the captives away from the authorities and send them to the safety of Canada.

On Wednesday, September 18, the legal proceedings began

in the Hartford courthouse. Judge Smith Thompson was presiding over the Circuit Court; Judge Judson had taken the Federal District Court seat for this period instead and was hearing civil claims.

The first order of business was the filing of the writ of habeas corpus by the counsel for the Africans. To excite the most interest and make the best case, counsel called on the marshal to bring the three little girls into court and show cause why they should not be released.

Lawyers Ralph I. Ingersoll and William Hungerford appeared for the Spanish government and Don José and Don Pedro. They said that at that moment the question of the status of the prisoners was being questioned in the libel that was being offered in District Court. There, lawyers for Lieutenant Commander Gedney were asking for salvage, and counsel for the Long Island claimants were asking for salvage and the doubloons that had so mysteriously disappeared.

Judge Thompson laid the case over until the following day. One of the Spaniards was sick and was not in court. All things considered, the judge needed a bit of time to decide whether or not the *Amistad* captives should be held for trial, turned over to federal authorities, or freed.

On Thursday, September 19, the complicated legal actions began to be unraveled. The courtroom was jammed with spectators. It was rumored that Judge Judson, like District Attorney Holabird, was the creature of the Administration and could be expected to rule in favor of the Spaniards, or at least of President Van Buren, who had asked that the slaves be held for his disposition.

Federal Marshal Wilcox brought Colonel Pendleton and the three little Negro girls into the courtroom. The girls were very much frightened by the strange surroundings and the sea of faces, and began to cry as soon as they entered. They swarmed over Colonel Pendleton, grasping with eager hands at this well-known figure, and weeping so loudly that they disturbed the court and had to be quieted. Colonel Pendleton tried to give them some fruit, but they were too upset to eat.

Finally the room was quiet enough for lawyer Ingersoll to be heard. First he read the writ of habeas corpus in behalf of the marshal. Then he read a warrant in behalf of the government against Singbe and others for murder and piracy, on which the little girls were ordered to pay $100 each to guarantee their appearance as witnesses; otherwise they were to be kept in jail. He also read the libel of Lieutenant Commander Gedney, which characterized the little girls as part of the cargo of the *Amistad;* the libel of Don Pedro Montes, which claimed the little girls as his slaves and valued them at $1,300; and the libel of the United States District Attorney, which stated that the Spanish government had demanded restoration of the property and asked the United States Attorney to try the Spanish claim.

If the court held that the captured Africans were property, they would be returned to the Spaniards. If it held that they were slaves illegally imported into the United States, they would be returned to Africa under provisions of the United States law, which stipulated repatriation of captured Africans by direction of the President.

When this last legal action was announced it aroused a furor among the spectators in the courtroom. The reason was obvious: it was the autumn of 1839 and the following year was election year. Tempers were already running hot, and the distaste for President Van Buren was very strong among Whigs and those who were not loyal Democrats. The President was always a politician, and he managed a long career in public life without often being pinned down to made any specific statement on great issues, and particularly on this specific issue of slavery, which was becoming so heated in discussion among the states in the 1830's.

One reason that Van Buren had obtained the nomination for the Presidency in 1836 was that he was a loyal Democrat from a Northern state, and some members of the party were growing restive under the succession of Southerners, who held such heavy power over the land through their appointed federal officials. Van Buren had managed to get the nomination without really committing himself on the subject of slavery and the extension of slave territory.

He behaved very shrewdly, "I acted the part of listener rather than that of a contestant," he said.[1] He had very little sympathy for those who feared the power of the South. "Respect for their source and the eloquence and earnestness with which they were made secured from me a close and interested attention, but they did not make the desired impression. My opinion was very decided that the Southern States had dealt with the subject of slavery, down to that period, in a wise and liberal spirit, and that they owed the disproportionate influence which they had possessed in the Federal government to other causes."

By 1839 Martin Van Buren was regarded as soft on slavery and had sacrificed the respect of the abolitionists, who believed that if Van Buren had his way, the *Amistad* captives would quietly be turned over to the Spaniards and returned to Havana to face death, or worse.

While the laywers for the *Amistad* captives had heard the story that the government was planning to interfere in its executive capacity, they had not been prepared for the case to take exactly the form it was taking. What they had hoped was that the writ of habeas corpus would be granted by the court, thus effectively outlawing all claims against the persons of the captives. But it was not to be done this way, they gathered in the courtroom. So the lawyer Seth Staples asked Judge Thompson for an adjournment until the following morning. It was granted.[2]

That night the three lawyers for the captives worked long and hard, trying to perfect what was, in effect, the defense of the slaves who had been brought north in the *Amistad*.

On Friday morning, September 20, they were as ready as they could hope to be, and they assembled in the courtroom, not

far from Hartford's State House, on the broad expanse of green
lawn so peaceful in appearance that it seemed unlikely men's
lives could be at stake there.

Theodore Sedgwick opened for the *Amistad* captives and
revealed the key point in the legal argument against returning
the Africans to the Spaniards or to anyone else.

Don Pedro Montes, in his action, had claimed that the little
girls were his private property, "legally purchased in the island
of Cuba, where slavery is allowed." According to his claim,
the girls should be delivered to him without loss, since the
United States and Spain were parties to a treaty guaranteeing
protection of the property of their nationals, when each happened to be in the territory of the other.

"Concedo licencia á tres negras ladinas, nombradas Juana,
Francisca, y Josefa, de la propriedad de Don Pedro Montes,
para que pasen á Puerto Principe por mar, debiendo presentarse
con esta al juez territorial respectivo." Thus read the passport
given Don Pedro and signed by Governor General Ezpeleta.

"I grant permission to three sound Negro women named
Juana, Francisca, and Josefa, belonging to Don Pedro Montes,
to go to Puerto Principe by sea, they being required to present
themselves before the respective territorial judges." So read the
translation offered the court.

Sedgwick attacked directly on this point. The little girls, he
said, were not then nor had they ever been slaves or the property
of Don Pedro Montes. They were native Africans, born in the
district of Senegambia. On April 20 they had been seized by
slavers (Don Pedro or his agents) and illegally put aboard a
Portuguese or Spanish vessel. Then they were taken to Cuba,
an act that was illegal because the Queen of Spain had acceded
to the treaty with Britain outlawing the importation of slaves
into Cuba. When the little girls were taken secretly to Cuba
they were hidden in a secret place, and kept there for two or
three weeks.

Then the girls were taken by stealth, at night, and put aboard the *Amistad*. They were at sea for two or three months and finally brought into New London where they were seized by the marshal of the District of Connecticut and imprisoned.

The burden of the Sedgwick argument was that the importation of the little girls from Africa was illegal in the first place under a decree of the King of Spain issued in 1817 and under a law promulgated by the Queen of Spain in 1838, and that there was no other basic issue.

He offered two affidavits; one by Augustus William Hansen, the other by John Ferry. These were two of the Africans brought to the New Haven jail by Lewis Tappan in his attempt to communicate with the *Amistad* captives. They swore that the little girls were native Africans, that the youngest was seven years old and the eldest nine years old, and that none of the three could speak Spanish or Portuguese. Lawyer Staples added that the marshal had in custody another of the *Amistad* Africans who had come to Cuba in the same vessel with the little girls and remembered them, and that he could be sworn and take an oath.

Ralph Ingersoll, counsel for the Spanish government, jumped up to object: "If the court please, I would make the suggestion whether your honors will go into this inquiry on the writ of habeas corpus while the merits of the case are pending before another tribunal, the District Court."

His point was that the Spaniards had filed in District Court for the return of the slaves as their property and that this question ought to be decided on its merits. He also pointed out that the Secretary of State had claimed they should be held because they should be returned to the Spanish under the treaty. And finally, if none of these, then the District Court should turn them over to the federal government for return to Africa as displaced Africans.

He made an emotional plea for the upholding of the letter of the law, and indicated that the whole spirit of American jurisprudence might lie in the balance. "Questions may arise, in the course of these trials, involving the faith of treaties and the rights of individuals, wherein great and manifest injustice might be done, if they are decided in this summary way as it would be impossible to go into all these questions on this summary process."[3]

All the while the adult *Amistad* captives were in the Hartford jail, awaiting the disposition of their case on the habeas corpus action. Only the three little girls were in court that day, and they did not understand a word of the proceedings.

What would happen to them?

Roger Baldwin appealed to the court (and to the public) when he pointed out that the girls were being held not as *people,* but as *property.* Now, he said, how long were they to be kept as "mere chattels"? Were they to be kept as long as the questions among the parties remain in the courts — perhaps a year, or five years?

And further, Baldwin said, if the District Court had really issued a warrant against the girls as property, they could not be seized as people and put in jail. But here they were in court, having been in jail.

The judge did not want to get into such legalisms at that moment. "There may be one branch of the [marshal's] return that will steer clear of these specifications — these persons are held under a commitment to appear as witnesses in a criminal case."

It was quite correct, the girls were also held as witnesses in the charge against the adult Africans for murder and piracy. Baldwin assured the court that the lawyers would offer bond for the girls, to be certain they appeared in court, and Judge Thompson said he was perfectly satisfied with that assurance.

The case was interrupted by a puzzled grand jury which filed into the room. The foreman addressed Judge Thompson: "May it please the court — I am directed to say that the Grand

Jury have before them a number of bills of indictment, charging certain persons with murder and piracy; and request of the Court a charge in relation to the law on that subject."

Judge Thompson could not explain the law until they had first explained to him the facts as they knew them, and at this moment the grand jury had no facts at all, nor any statement about what was supposed to have occurred on board the *Amistad*. He sent the jury back to get a statement of facts from the United States District Attorney's office. Then and only then, said Judge Thompson, could the Circuit Court decide whether or not it had jurisdiction in this case.

In some confusion the grand jurors retired. They came back not long afterward, having been presented with a statement of facts. The statement told the story, generally speaking, but showed confusion about the little-known status of slaves in Cuba, referring to the 53 Negroes aboard the *Amistad* as "*ladinos* (that is — not natives of Cuba)."

When the foreman finished reading the statement, he asked the court to instruct the grand jury in the law. "Is this the only business you have before you?" asked Judge Thompson.

"It is," replied the foreman.

Judge Thompson then promised to examine the facts and to instruct the grand jury on the law in the afternoon session. The jury filed out of the courtroom, and Roger Baldwin continued his argument for release of the little girls on the writ of habeas corpus.

Judge Judson was sitting with Judge Thompson on this day on the Circuit Court, and he listened with particular interest to the argument. Seldom had the abolitionists been offered a more clear-cut opportunity to make the case against trading in human beings in a place where law was administered. They had been effectively cut off from making that case in the place where the laws of the nation were made by the Gag Rule of the House of Representatives. They had the feeling that President Van Buren and his entire establishment were opposed to them and favorable to the traffic in slaves. In any event the activities of the executive branch offered very little outside election years in the way of platforms from which the full attention of the electorate might be attracted.

The *Amistad* affair, however, gave the abolitionists of New England and New York exactly what they wanted, for from the initial report of the sinister long, low, black schooner that lay off the United States shores the *Amistad* had been cloaked in mystery and was an attraction for Americans everywhere. As a sturdy advocate of human rights, Roger Baldwin was determined not to lose this chance to put his arguments into the public records of the United States.

Baldwin addressed himself to the issue — moral and legal — of the status of the *Amistad* captives. Not only did he intend to persuade the court to consider this matter on its legal grounds, he also wished to make sure that the full horror of considering human beings as *property* be brought forth.

At first, he said, the only matter before the District Court had been Judge Judson's order to hold the *Amistad* and her cargo. *After* the writ of habeas corpus had been devised, the other parties had come forth "thinking thereby to deprive these interesting but friendless children of the benefit of the writ of habeas corpus."

Roger Baldwin did not mention President Van Buren. He did not have to mention him. His audience understood perfectly.

Baldwin began by lacing into Lieutenant Commander Gedney, not forgetting to characterize him as an officer of the United States Navy, making quite certain that the audience and readers would see the anomaly of Gedney's position. Having been told that the Africans were slaves, said Baldwin, "this Lieutenant Gedney thought proper to take these persons, a large part of whom were not on board the vessel at the time, but on shore, and bring them into the port of New London; and now he presses in this court the claim that he had rendered a 'meritorious service' not to these poor Africans, by saving their lives, but by reducing them to the condition of slavery, men who, when he found them, were free; and he asks the District Court to award him salvage on these human beings, for the 'meritorious service' he had performed in reducing them to bondage."

The contempt in Baldwin's voice was unmistakable.

He had no quarrel with Lieutenant Commander Gedney's claim to salvage of the cargo of the *Amistad,* but he asked that the Distirct Court of the State of Connecticut "not reduce men to slavery when they were found in a state of freedom — not for any purpose whatsoever.[4]

Baldwin reviewed the circumstances of the capture of the African children. His voice was heavy with sarcasm as he referred again and again to the "Spanish gentlemen": "And upon the mere suggestion that these individuals are claimed as the slaves of certain *Spanish gentlemen,* are we to set aside our own laws, and those of every civilized nation, who have long held this trade to be piratical and infamous?"

He reviewed the outlawry of the slave trade. "What pretence then is there," he asked, "for the assumption of jurisdiction of these persons *as property,* when, by the laws of the whole civilized world, they cannot be reduced to the condition of property without the commission of a felony?"

He reminded the court that these slaves had been brought from Africa so recently that they did not even speak civilized tongues.

"Suppose they were Englishmen or Spaniards, seized under a process claiming *salvage* for saving them from the wreck of an Algerine corsair." Baldwin continued, working to a point: How could the court distinguish, he asked, between such a case and that of the Africans, when it had already been proved that they were brought into the United States in violation of *Spanish* laws and when they could not even be legally held in Spain as slaves?

The Africans' lawyer also questioned Lieutenant Commander

Gedney's right to pick up the *Amistad* captives from New York soil and transfer them to Connecticut jurisdiction.

Baldwin made sure it was in the record that Gedney had valued the slaves, as *property*, at $25,000. He also made sure that auditors and readers would remember that they were in the free state of Connecticut: "Lieutenant Gedney says he found these Negroes in the possession of the vessel. Then, when they were found, the presumption was that they were free; for, the gentlemen will not find, in this state, the law of slavery that every colored man is presumed to be a slave, until the contrary is shown. Here, thank God, the law presumes that every man is free."[5]

The question to be decided, the New Haven lawyer averred, was whether the slaves were people or property. If they were human beings, then the District Court had no jurisdiction over them and they must be freed.

As he warmed to his subject, Baldwin returned to the castigation of Lieutenant Commander Gedney as an American naval officer, a representative of the people, "for reducing to the condition of slavery men and children whom he found free in fact."

He gave a picture of American naval officers coming into American courts, claiming rewards for capturing slaves, and referred to "these Spanish slave dealers, whom he [Gedney] chooses to denominate *gentlemen!*"

The day before, in District Court, Judge Judson had called on the lawyers representing Gedney to show why the slaves, or former slaves, or captives, should be sold as property. He remarked at that time that there was no power in the District Court to sell men, women, and children.

Here Judge Thompson interrupted the proceedings.

"If that be so, they are not taken nor held at all under the process of that Court for salvage and it is unnecessary to argue that question."

Judge Judson did not want to take so much responsibility, particularly in view of President Van Buren's desire that the

Negroes be held for the executive department's decisions. "Yesterday the Court had very little time; but I meant to intimate distinctly that the District Court had no power to sell these persons."

Judge Thompson would no let it go at that: "The simple question before this court is, whether there are any legal questions pending, to justify the Court in holding them. It is a mere question as to the liberties of these persons."

Judge Judson hastened to amplify his statements: "Perhaps I should say that was the annunciation of my opinion — all the process in the District Court is the libel of the United States Government, claiming to hold them on the claim of the Spanish Minister, and of the United States law, and the libel of Don Pedro Montes, claiming the restoration of these persons as his slaves."[6]

Roger Baldwin bored in at this point to repeat and strengthen his arguments. He reminded the court of the laws against slave traffic and again brought up the comparison of whites captured by an Algerine corsair. What if Don Pedro Montes had been so captured, he asked; would any court in Christendom return Don Pedro to Berber slavery after he escaped, simply because of a treaty with one of the Barbary powers? He went on:

> Don Pedro Montes comes here himself as a man who is encouraging this foul traffic, by purchasing of the slaver. How much better is the man who purchases the stolen property than the man who steals it? But here are stolen men, brought in by pirates, purchased by this man — how much better is he to be regarded in the Court than if the original slaver had been brought here? Would the Court allow the claim of the man who stole these human beings from Africa if he should come here and ask the Court to restore these persons to him as his property? I say this man has not more right of property in these men than the orginal slaver. His claim is founded on gross injustice; and he himself does not deny that he has abetted the enterprise by purchasing the property. I say then, in regard to his claim, from

the place where they were when his libel was filed, and from the very character of his claim, it is utterly impossible it should be allowed in the District Court of this State.[7]

Baldwin then proceeded to consider the actions of the United States district attorney in behalf of the federal government, and in a manner calculated to inflame the abolitionists:

> I ask, what right has the District Attorney of the United States to file a libel in the District Court of the State of Connecticut and cause to be apprehended as slaves or to be held subject to further proceedings these persons, simply because the Spanish minister has thought proper to make the demand for their restoration . . .
>
> What law has imposed upon the executive of the United States the obligation to hunt up the runaway slaves of Spanish subjects, and restore them?
>
> . . . Is it thereby made the duty of the Governors of our Free States, upon the demand of the minister of Spain, to issue a warrant and arrest the fugitive slave and deliver him up?[8]

He turned then to the other claim of the federal government: "that the *Amistad* captives be held until the court ascertained whether or not they were entitled to freedom, and that they then be delivered to the President of the United States to be transported to Africa as free men."[9]

Baldwin's point was that the law cited therein concerned only slaves brought into the United States. The *Amistad* people were not slaves when they came to the United States, they were captives of those who had participated in enslaving them. Consequently, there was absolutely no reason for the federal government to try to enter the case. The *Amistad* captives should be set free, as free men.

Ralph Ingersoll, counsel for the Spanish, arose to take violent exception to Baldwin's constant reference to the Spaniards as slave dealers and pirates. And he came quickly to his point: "Again we have been told that these persons cannot be considered as property, because this is a free country. We are before a Court acting for a peculiar kind of government. In a part of these States, slaves are recognized as property. It is idle for the gentleman to stand here and say they are *persons* and therefore not *property.*"[10]

Ingersoll continued: "The suggestion that these claimants were ever engaged in the African slave trade, or that they knew any persons that are so engaged, or that they knew these persons to have been brought from Africa is utterly unfounded and entirely gratuitous. They stand precisely as the inhabitants of nine of these States now stand."

So Ingersoll had brought the issue into the open: the Spanish gentlemen were just the same as American Southerners, holding slaves legally (and without looking closely into whence they had came, as custom dictated). The manner in which Ingersoll put the issue laid it out in terms that showed every Southern sympathizer, every slaveholder in the United States, that his interests were bound up in the *Amistad* case. The words also inflamed every advocate of abolition with new fires.

Seth Staples of New York, one of the ardent lawyers for the *Amistad* captives, made the final statement before noon recess that day, trying to bring the *Amistad* back into focus:

> There may be certain indications which might be recognized as evidence of persons being in the condition of property in the Island of Cuba; but I know that our laws look at this matter in another light. Yet, we are here called upon to divert our attention from the main object of this writ — to turn our eye from this real transaction and shift it off as a matter which concerns goods and chattels, because here are questions pending about property. Gentlemen, go on with your litigation, as to the *Amistad* and her cargo, to your hearts' content; but take not these children and deprive them of habeas corpus, under pretext of a question whether they are brutes or human beings.[11]

That was the end of the morning session.

8/The Trial of the Captives II

As is so often the case in complicated legal matters, the question of the habeas corpus request was far more than the simple matter it appeared to be, and all concerned were well aware of the real issues beneath the surface.

In reporting the first part of the trial, the Hartford *Courant* put it in perspective from the abolitionist point of view: "The plea on which the District Attorney asks for the children is an anomalous one. They are first to be treated as slaves in order that they may be made free — but we have no right, said the learned advocate [Staples] to detain them in durance one hour, they are as free as the atmosphere we breathe."[1]

Actually, the reporter's words were more a reflection of his and the newspaper's hopes than anything that had happened in court that morning. "We think," Ingersoll had said, that "this court will not, in this summary manner, take the case out of the District Court" — where it was to be decided on the basis of the various questions of property and federal intervention.

From the standpoint of the judge there was a good deal to be considered during the luncheon hour, and not the least of these considerations was the request of the President of the United States that he be allowed to have final say about the fate of the captives. The President did not make such requests lightly.

And Martin Van Buren particularly was not prone to interfere in various government processes without good reasons of his own. Had the *Amistad* case been simply a matter of concern between the Spanish Don José and Don Pedro on the one hand and the captives on the other, it would have been easy enough for President Van Buren to stall his answer to the Spanish minister and then, after the case was decided, to offer his regrets that it had been decided before he could act. He had, in fact, set such wheels in motion with his delay in replying to Don Amgel's first communication.

No, it was apparent in the President's unusual interference in the court processes that he had an abiding interest in the *Amistad* case. Therefore, it was important that the case be adjudged in such a manner as to bind off backlash.

The judge had another question to ponder at luncheon: Were the *Amistad* captives to be tried for murder and piracy? The Spanish government, of course, said that the United States government had no jurisdiction in the case. Would that be the decision of the court?

When Judge Thompson returned from luncheon, the grand jury was called in to hear what he had to say on the subject of the law governing the facts of the *Amistad*'s seizure by the blacks. In the first place, if the United States federal courts had any right to try the *Amistad* captives for murder and piracy, the trial would have had to be held in a New York district court, for they were apprehended in New York waters, not Connecticut waters. But that was not the important matter, said Judge Thompson; what was important was that, in his view, the United States government had no right to try the *Amistad* captives because whatever they did was done aboard a Spanish vessel with a Spanish crew and commander and Spanish papers, bound on a coasting voyage in Spanish waters. Therefore, there were no grounds for trial of the *Amistad* captives for murder or mutiny or piracy.

The grand jury was dismissed.

The court returned to hearing of the arguments for and
against the granting of the writ of habeas corpus in behalf of
the *Amistad* children.

Lawyer Staples moved quickly to make a very important
point in the matter of the *Amistad* captives, and particularly
of the children. He knew, he said, that slavery was so corrupted
that although the trade was outlawed by the Spanish Crown,
slaves were constantly landed in Cuba under false pretenses,
and that they were moved about freely. He went on:

> But the question here is, who are these children? Whence came
> they? On this subject we have an African, a colored man, an in-
> terpreter, who has been with these children and examined them;
> and he says they are native Africans. . . .
>
> Well, if these children were born in Africa, they were not old
> enough to have been brought into the Island of Cuba before
> the law abolishing the slave trade. If the African question is settled
> they must have been brought to Cuba since the treaty of 1827. . . .
>
> We have the highest possible evidence, not direct, that these
> children were born and bred in Africa, where and where only,
> they could have learned the dialect they now speak; and that they
> were brought to Cuba after the treaty alluded to; so that, im-
> mediately after they reached the Island of Cuba, they were free;
> and no subsequent purchase could make them slaves.

Staples then attacked the question that interested everyone
in America: Why was the United States government concerning itself with this case?

> Now as to the claim of the District Attorney:
>
> 1. He acts here in some manner in aid of the movements of
> the minister of Spain. How we know not.
>
> 2. He acts for the Executive of the U.S. on the supposition
> that these Africans may, in some respects, fall into his hands.
> On that subject the law is perfectly clear. If these slaves were not
> brought in here by American citizens, or in American vessels,
> the President of the United States has nothing to do with them. . . .

But it has been supposed that the President has something to do with these persons in consequence of articles of treaty. So far from this, it is decidedly the other way. . . . The sixth article of the treaty provides for the mutual protection of each other's vessels in each other's jurisdiction. Now, in what method is this to be done? Through the courts of justice. . . .[2]

Staples carried the argument that afternoon, although Roger Baldwin rose at least once to read a letter expounding a point of law before the court. One important part of the *Amistad* captives' case, obviously, was to prove that these were Africans, not Cuban slaves and sons of slaves. To this end, an affidavit was introduced from one of the captives in the Hartford jail, relative to the children of the *Amistad*. It was dated Hartford, September 20, 1839, and it read:

Affidavit of Bahoo

I, Bahoo, of Bandaboo in Africa, being duly cautioned, depose and say that I knew Marngroo and Kenyee, two little girls now in prison at Hartford; they were born at Bandaboo, in Mandingo, and came over on the same vessel that I did to Havana, as did Penna and the little boy Carre; that they were about two moons in coming from Africa to Havana, where they staid less than one moon. Good many in the vessel, and many died — were tight together, two and two chained together by hands and feet, night and day, until near Havana, when the chains were taken off — were landed on the coast at a little place near sun set — stayed until night, and walked into the city, put them in an old building and fastened them in — after some time the people now in jail were put on board the same vessel they came here in, in the night, and sailed away about the time the gun fired. I know that these children are the same that came over from Africa, and that Marngroo and Kenyee were born in the same place I was, which was Bandaboo, and further saith not.

Bahoo his X mark[3]

Staples then made direct reference to President Van Buren, wondering why he had interested himself in this case: "If a claim is made for delivering up these persons, it must be upon the Executive of the State of Connecticut; and I presume the present Executive of the United States, with his characteristic caution, will not move in this matter."

He suggested that he would like to know more about the authority under which the District Attorney filed his libel. District Attorney Holabird replied that the order came from the United States Secretary of State.

Judge Thompson seemed inclined to consider whether or not the *Amistad* captives should be released. "The great difficulty," he said, "laying out of view all these questions of libels, they are now in the custody of the law, and what is to be done with them? I should be glad to have some answer to this question."

Staples said that if they had done nothing against the law, nothing could be done with them. "I consider that they did not come at all in violation of the law. If they did, the President would have a right to interfere. But they have been brought into Court as property."

Judge Thompson pursued: "My object is really to get information. If they are dismissed what provision will be made for them? They stand here without any criminal process against them. According to the laws of the State of Connecticut, is there any authorized provision for their support?"

Mr. Staples answered: "They would be provided for as foreign paupers. The citizens of Connecticut would be very cautious about delivering them up to any pretended friends, who might possibly stop short of Africa. But the State of Connecticut is bound to take care of them. But they are not to be holden by the laws, under these circumstances."

The judge appeared to be satisfied with this explanation that the Negroes would not simply be cast adrift if released by the courts. There was never any question of the future of the Negroes, actually, because once the American Anti-Slavery Society took an interest in them, they became the current national heroes of the abolitionists, and there was no shortage of moneys available for them.

Another affidavit was introduced, that of John Ferry, the Negro interpreter, who backed up that of Bahoo of Mandingo.

Ralph Ingersoll, attorney for the Spaniards, undertook to question the interpreter, attempting to cast doubt on his ability to communicate with the Africans. He got nowhere with the attempt. Ferry said he knew the languages of the area well because he made it a point to travel around the West Indies seeking out plantations where people spoke those languages.

William Hungerford, second counsel for the Spaniards, then appealed to the court not to enter into the merits of the case in this action, which was to discover if there was any conceivable reason for holding the Africans. His objection was not accepted by the court, which ordered the investigation to continue.

District Attorney Holabird then arose to explain the government's position. He dismissed the matter of the Spanish treaty in a sentence or two — apparently having noted how little effect this had on the court and how ill an effect it was having on the public — and relied upon the second part of his argument: that the Negroes should be kept in the United States to await the disposition of the President because an American law might have been violated. The President would then send the slaves back to Africa where they belonged. He went on:

> How does this matter present itself? Here is a vessel freighted with Africans. They, at the time they were discovered, had control of the vessel. As to the national character of that vessel, I contend nothing is yet known. Nothing is more common than for a slave vessel to sail under false colors. We can, in the District Court, go into this question. For aught this tribunal knows, this will prove to be an American vessel. Then I say that this inquiry as to the true character of this vessel is the proper province of the District Court. I believe that on examination of the libel, it will be found to bring the case within the province of that law, if the fact appear that the vessel is owned by American citizens.

And District Attorney Holabird read with great gravity from the libel he had prepared. Here he was guilty of outright dishonesty. In his original letter to Secretary of State Forsyth he had not questioned the nationality of the long, low, black schooner. He had said: "The marshal of this district has in custody the Spanish schooner *Amistad*," and he had wanted the Secretary to dispose of the Negroes in some manner that would not make it necessary for him to bring them into court.[4]

Then, in his second letter, on September 9, District Attorney Holabird had been even more forthright. He referred to his previous letter.[5] "Since then," he said, "I have made a further examination of the law on the subject of the jurisdiction of our courts, which has brought me fully to the conclusion, that the courts neither of this nor of any other district of the United States can take cognizance of any offense they have committed, as the offense by them committed was done and committed on board a vessel belonging exclusively to citizens of a foreign state: and they [the blacks] not being citizens of the United States, the vessel having a national character at the time the offence was committed."

District Attorney Holabird had shown his feelings certainly in that letter of September 9: "I would respectfully inquire, sir, whether there are no treaty stipulations with the Government of Spain that would authorize our Government to deliver them up to the Spanish authorities. And, if so, whether it could be done before our court sits."[6]

Now, on this third day of the court's consideration of the *Amistad* cases, Holabird was trying to reverse himself. He was obviously serving President and party, and not his conscience or the unbiased cause of justice.

District Attorney Holabird denied that the United States government was acting in behalf of the Spaniards. In this he was correct: the Administration was acting in its own behalf, seeing a vital election issue in the *Amistad* affair, and attempting desperately to keep it from becoming a clear-cut case of the rights of black men. To let the case drag on and become clear would hurt Martin Van Buren grievously. If the Negroes were released by the courts, the white slaveholders of the South would be infuriated and would distrust the Administration. If the Negroes were held by the courts and returned to the custody of the Spaniards, the abolitionists would be infuriated. But on the whole Martin Van Buren found his lot to be more easily cast with the slaveholders than with the abolitionists. Electoral votes were what counted in elections, not popular votes; and it was possible for a man to win the election with a minority of the total votes cast. Further, Van Buren must first secure the Presidential nomination again if he was to succeed himself, and as matters stood that meant winning two-thirds of the votes in the Democratic national convention. To win two-thirds majority of the Democratic convention in 1840 a man had to be popular in the South. Martin Van Buren, hand-picked successor to President Andrew Jackson, *was* popular in the South, and he intended to remain so. He was losing popularity in the nation every day because of his refusal to come to grips with issues. He retained control of much of the Democratic party machinery, but this could be upset, and the upset could come from the organized slave-owners more easily than from the only partly organized abolitionists.

The legal arguments continued. Lawyer Staples asked District Attorney Holabird how he could maintain that the slaves had been brought into the United States illegally, if he did not file any charges against anyone for having brought them in illegally. The District Attorney avoided that unpleasant point.

The lawyers for the Spaniards knew that they would have to make a case for themselves in this proceeding and could not rely on moving the matter to the District Court, where there would be a strong presumption that the Negroes were property and it would have to be proved that they were not. They called the cabin boy Antonio to attempt to invalidate the affidavit of Bahoo to the effect that the little girls were Africans and not Spanish slaves from Cuba.

Since Antonio could speak no European language but Spanish, Lieutenant Meade was brought into court as interpreter. He was sworn, then he explained the oath in Spanish to Antonio, and was again sworn. Then Antonio testified.[7]

His testimony did not prove much, except that the little girls were well treated aboard the *Amistad* and were allowed the freedom of the decks. He — led by the lawyers — made much of the fact that the *Amistad* lay in plain sight of several British cruisers while in port at Havana and that these cruisers saw the girls and other Negroes and did not bother the captain of the *Amistad*.

Baldwin cross-examined Antonio and determined that the girls could not speak Spanish and that they said they had come from Africa.

"Do you know that they came from Africa in any other way than that they told you so?" asked lawyer Ingersoll for the Spaniards, trying to show that the evidence was mere hearsay.

"They told me so," said Antonio.[8]

The really knotty issue — and this is where the case of the abolitionists was very weak — was in the treaty between the United States and Spain, which said that *all* property of Spanish citizens was to be surrendered to them in case of piracy or shipwreck or other trouble. There was no exception for slaves. And, although many Americans disliked the recollection, the United States recognized slavery as lawful and proper in 1839. The abolitionists could say that it was immoral, inhuman, and improper, but the law of the land said otherwise.

Lawyer Hungerford used this issue skillfully in his case for the Spaniards. He reproved the counsel for the Africans because they cast doubts on the reputation of Don Pedro. If Don Pedro were a slaveholder in a land where slaveholding was proper, why should anyone chide him? If Don Pedro owned slaves, which he had acquired lawfully, why should he not attempt to seek their return to him?

Throughout the case counsel on both sides cited the case of the ship *Antelope*, which had been working between Africa and the Americas early in the nineteenth century. During the Colombian revolution against Spain in the 1820's an American-owned ship was commissioned as a privateer to capture Spanish vessels. It went out, *in violation of American neutrality,* and happened to capture a number of slave ships. It was captured, brought to an American port, and libeled by the captain of another ship. The United States filed a claim to free the Negroes. The Spanish and Portuguese consulates filed claims in behalf of the owners of the slaves on the ship, who had been captured from other ships. The privateer's claim was dismissed. The American claim was dismissed because the slaves were regarded as property, and they were returned to the owners. The case went to the Supreme Court of the United States, which split, and thus the original judgment stood.

The United States was in a difficult legal position in any matter involving slavery, and was trying to take the high moral position that slave trading was improper but slaveholding was not. The *Antelope* case had proved to be a victory for slaveholders. Those in sympathy with the status quo were hopeful that the *Amistad* would not prove to be a reversal.

After hearing arguments all day on Friday, Judge Thompson adjourned the court until Saturday morning.

That night the lawyers speculated on the decision. From Judge Thompson they believed they would have no particular bias. He had not shown any indication of such bias in the past or now. Judge Judson was more suspect: he had been the lawyer in a case in Connecticut in which a Negro girl was expelled from the white Ladies Academy operated by Prudence Crandall. He had acted as more than counsel: he had been a member of a committee of the citizens of Canterbury, who called on Miss Crandall to protest the admission of Sarah Harris, the Negro girl. Miss Crandall's white students had quit the school, for while New Englanders, by and large, stood for equality of the blacks before the law, they did not wish to rub shoulders with them.

Judson had also been active in winning passage of a Connecticut law that prohibited the establishment of schools for Negroes without the permission of the town selectmen, and Judson, as prosecutor in Windham County Court, had tried the case of Prudence Crandall, winning public acclaim for his attacks on the Negroes. The law stood, but juries would not convict under the law. So it was a Pyrrhic victory for the prosecutor, which made him a controversial character on the matter of black equality. The abolitionist lawyers expected no justice from him.

On Saturday morning Judge Thompson took the bench and spoke to counsel for both parties.

The case was very difficult, he said, because none of the prisoners could be accused of any criminal act under the American system. The issue to be decided was whether the District Court could hold the prisoners on a legal charge. If so, they must be held. If not, they must be discharged by the Circuit Court. But "great injustice" might be done to some parties (the Spaniards) if the prisoners were summarily discharged. After all, if the prisoners did not like the decision of the District Court, they could appeal to the Circuit Court and then to the Supreme Court.

"It has been argued by the counsel for the prisoners," Judge Thompson said, "that no court of justice can entertain the right of property in human beings. But slavery, or the right of controlling the freedom of a certain class of men, is not only sanctioned by foreign powers, with whom we have treaties, but is recognized by the Supreme Court of our own country."[9]

The only question, said Judge Thompson, was whether the property involved was rightly in the possession of the District Court — in other words, there could be a right of property in the Africans, a right held by the Spaniards, and the United States government must recognize that right if it existed.

He said the prisoners could *not* be taken out of the jurisdiction of the District Court on the writ of habeas corpus. (They were not, therefore, persons, as distinct from property.) He asked the lawyers to argue the question: Did the District Court have jurisdiction in the case over this property?

Judge Thompson was not arbitrary or injudicious. He offered the counsel for both sides all the time they needed, hoping he could finish that afternoon, but prepared to lay the case over until later if necessary.

But there was no need for long hours of preparation. The abolitionist lawyers had lost the battle they wished to fight — the battle of humanity. They had hoped to obtain the judgment that Negroes were people. Such a judgement would have rung loud and clear throughout the American landscape, seven years before the beginning of the famous Dred Scott case in Missouri.

Judge Thompson wanted counsel to delay the case.

Lawyer Ingersoll suggested that counsel for each side furnish the court with a brief, so that the judge could give an opinion at some future time. This would give Judge Thompson leisure to consult his law books and write an opinion that would be studded with learned references.

Lawyer Staples said the counsel for the Africans would confer during the luncheon recess and would then be prepared to say whether they would accept this idea or insist on arguing the case that day.

Meanwhile arrangements were made by counsel for the Africans to file a writ of habeas corpus for all the other African prisoners, just to make the case good and tight in the event of appeal to the United States Supreme Court.

The court recessed at noon. And lawyers Baldwin, Staples, and Sedgwick conferred among themselves with officials of the American Anti-Slavery Society and other abolitionists. They decided to stick to the issue, expecting, however, that they had lost this first round. The issue, as they saw it, was that the *Amistad* prisoners were not slaves and had never been slaves, but were kidnaped Africans, who deserved to be treated as free men and returned to their country. Neither the Spaniards nor the United States government had the right to interfere with them. As for Lieutenant Commander Gedney, he might libel the cargo all he wished, but he had best leave the people alone.

The lawyers returned to the court at two o'clock in the afternoon.

Judge Thompson took his seat.

Had the opposing counsel come to any agreement with respect to briefs? he asked.

Ingersoll said they had not come to agreement. There was a difference of opinion. As far as the counsel for the Spaniards and the United States government were concerned, they were willing to present briefs and let the judge take his time.

Roger Baldwin arose. They wished to press the question of the habeas corpus for an immediate decision. It was unfair to the prisoners to do anything but seek their immediate freedom.

Staples remarked that it would be much more convenient for him to present a brief and accommodate the judge, but he, too, felt that the needs of the Africans were paramount.

Judge Thompson decided in favor of the counsel for the imprisoned Africans.

But, Roger Baldwin pursued, did the District Court have jurisdiction over the Africans.

Judge Thompson replied that that was a simple question, and he hoped counsel for both sides would bear it in mind as they argued.

Baldwin briefly summarized the arguments he had made earlier, the net being that he did not believe the courts had jurisdiction over the *Amistad* captives.

William Hungerford argued for the Spaniards that whether the Africans were people or property was a question for the District Court to decide, and Ingersoll carried that further by indicating that it had already been shown they were property.

District Attorney Holabird announced that he had been thinking about the case. "I stand here to contend that these blacks are freemen — that they have been brought within the jurisdiction of the United States, and may be holden to abide the decision of the proper authority, and if found to be, as I suppose, native Africans, they may be sent to their native land."

Of all those arguing, Holabird was met with the most suspicion. The positions and motivations of the others were apparent, but District Attorney Holabird had boxed the compass as much as the *Amistad* ever did, yet he had not been of any assistance to the Africans nor had he changed his position that the District Court ought to hold the *Amistad* captives for trial.

Seth Staples, who was an ardent young abolitionist, interjected a note of high emotion into the proceedings during his argument:

> It must be shown that there is a treaty requiring us to restore Africans to slave holders at Cuba when they have been purchased contrary to the laws of Spain.
>
> Let such a claim be set up by the President, Senate, or Spanish Minister, let the government of this nation avow that they will surrender these victims of oppression, and I will abandon such a country and seek my fortunes in some British island!
>
> Corruption is, I know, stalking abroad in this land; doctrines are set up that are contrary to the principles of our government; and violence is threatened to those who contend for impartial liberty and the rights of man — yet I do not believe we are so far gone as to be slave-catchers for foreign claimants.

The argument continued, Staples holding the floor the rest of the afternoon, and occasionally waxing emotional as he fought for the Africans. He went on until seven o'clock in the evening, when Judge Thompson, deciding they could not possibly finish, so adjourned the court until Monday.

District Attorney Holabird wrote to Secretary of State Forsyth, revealing his feelings and some actions unknown to the public. Before court had opened on Wednesday he had appeared at Judge Thompson's chambers, because he had just received the note from the Secretary of State requesting that the Africans be held at all costs. The judge had heard him without comment, so the district attorney hoped he had accomplished the task. But when Circuit Court had opened, the judge had not charged the jury to find a cause for trial of the Africans for murder or piracy, and Holabird had been forced to scurry about to place the facts before the jurors. He had filed other libels in the District Court — in other words, he had done his duty, trying to be sure the Negroes were held on one charge or another.

The district attorney also misquoted Judge Thompson in the letter to Secretary Forsyth, indicating that the judge had held that the court had jurisdiction over offenses the Negroes might have committed on board the *Amistad,* when in fact the judge had said exactly the opposite.

District Attorney Holabird's position was very simple: he believed the Negroes were slaves, pirates, and murderers, and this belief stood out clearly in his correspondence.[10] He did not refer to the lawyers or to the principals in the case, but to "the writ . . . prayed out in this court . . . by Tappan &c." Writer and reader were of the same mind — they believed in slavery and were struggling against an abolitionist who was their sworn enemy, Lewis Tappan, driving force behind the movement to free the Africans.

On Monday, September 23, Judge Thompson took the bench again, having considered the problem over the weekend — and he did just what everyone expected him to do, for he had already warned of his thinking on Friday. He denied the motions of habeas corpus on the grounds that the District Court did have jurisdiction over the *Amistad* captives if they were slaves, and that remained to be decided. The questions of property rights in slaves had been decided before, particularly in the case of the *Antelope,* which he found to be directly in point.

"My feelings," said Judge Thompson, "are personally as abhorrent to the system of slavery as those of any man here, but I must, on my oath, pronounce what the laws are on this subject. The true question, then, is as to the law, and not as to any of the questions involved in this case."

It was clear to him that the laws of the United States did provide that slaves were property, that the treaty with Spain did provide that property should be returned to the Spaniards, that if the District Court of Connecticut did not have jurisdiction over the salvage claim of Lieutenant Commander Gedney (which he believed it did have) then the District Court of New York would have jurisdiction.

Judge Thompson rejected the heroic issue, the issue of liberty: "It has been said that this is a question of liberty, and therefore that this court ought to decide the case in a summary and prompt manner. But in the judgment of the court, this ought to have no influence on the decision."

He therefore refused to rule on the questions of the facts, except to deny the writ of habeas corpus.

Roger Baldwin asked the court, with some heat, if this decision meant that a foreigner coming to the United States with a slave could call upon the courts to enforce his claim to the slave.

Judge Thompson would not be trapped. As a judge, he said, he did not feel called upon to decide on that abstract question. His implication was clearly that the District Court would hear the facts and pass judgment on them in view of the laws of the land.

The case was then referred across the way to the District Court, where Judge Andrew T. Judson presided. Judge Judson directed United States Attorney Holabird to go to Montauk in a revenue cutter to investigate the conditions under which the *Amistad* had been seized and to report back to him. The court was adjourned until the third Tuesday in November, when it was to reconvene in Hartford. Marshal Norris Wilcox was ordered to see that the prisoners were cared for properly.

Judge Judson said he would entertain a motion to discharge the prisoners from jail if they could give bail (he was particularly embarrassed about keeping the children in jail), but counsel for the *Amistad* captives noted that since they were being detained as property and not persons, to permit them to take bail would be to set valuation on property and to play into the hands of the Spaniards.

9/Waiting

The *Amistad* captives were scarcely aware of what was occurring in the Circuit and District Courts of Hartford. The little
girls had been in court much of the time, but the men had been
confined to the jail.

From the moment the captives arrived in Hartford they attracted the attention of all New England. In the first three days of
their stay more than 3,000 people came to the jail, to pay 12½
cents apiece for a look at the captives. The jailers assured the
spectators that the money would be used to defray the expenses
of keeping the Africans, and then for luxuries for them to eat
and wear.

As the trial continued, and the newspapers reported the arguments in whichever bias they preferred, public interest grew
greater. People soon began coming from miles around; one man
said he had traveled 100 miles just to see them.[1] New York
newspapers sent special correspondents to report the trial and
carried long articles detailing the various legal debates advanced.

Others, like Thomas Gallaudet, founder of a school for the
deaf and dumb in Connecticut, took an interest in the welfare
of the prisoners. He worked out a sign language with the Africans. The need for communication was becoming apparent to all
those who had dealings with the Africans because none of the

interpreters was a fellow tribesman and none spoke their native tongues. Some communication was possible, largely through the language of the Gallinas valley, but it was limited. The search for proper translators continued.

The *Amistad* captives went back to New Haven in September, back to the jail across from the lush grass of the town green. From the date of the trial, they were treated much more humanely than earlier, partly because of the efforts of their abolitionist friends, but also because the criminal charges against them had been quashed. The marshal and his assistant were used to dealing with escaped Negro slaves, with misbehaving Negro freedmen, and with tough whites; but in the *Amistad* captives they had an entirely different group — independent people who had not been enslaved long enough to become subservient, men who had risen against those who called themselves "masters" and struck them down, rebels who had been willing to fight and die for their freedom.

The prisoners, except for Singbe, were taken back in one group in a canal boat. Singbe was transported separately, but he was soon placed with the other prisoners in the bigger, airier apartments above the first floor. No longer was there a charge of murder or piracy hanging over him. The worst that could happen to him, and to the others, would be to be adjudged the property of the Spaniards and returned to them. But Singbe could expect to be taken to Havana and tried, and probably killed in some particularly horrible fashion to serve as an example to the other slaves of Spain's disintegrating colonial empire.

Soon the captives were seen disporting themselves on the New Haven green, where they were taken almost daily by Colonel Pendleton for exercise. They turned somersaults and played leaping games, much to the amusement of the white spectators who came to watch the African savages.

People continued to come from far and near to see the captives in the jail. Phrenologists came to feel their heads and to argue about their qualities of character. In the absence of any real communication the speculations and arguments were many. Dr. R.H. Collyer came, accompanied by Lieutenant Meade, who had developed a very personal interest in the fate of the captives, although he did not much care for them. When the doctor wished to take calipers to measure Singbe's head, Meade ordered Singbe to take off his hat and submit.

What happened next was a measure of the relationship between the *Amistad* captives and the outside world at the beginning of October, 1839.

1. Singbe flatly refused to take off his hat or lower his head.

2. Lieutenant Meade grabbed him by the head and neck and forced him to submit.

3. Doctor Collyer and his companions pleaded that perhaps the intercession of some of the abolitionists might make things easier for all.[2]

Lieutenant Meade's treatment of Singbe was occasioned not so much by personal choleric temperament as by the lieutenant's refusal to regard the Africans as people. He held the view that these were slaves and therefore inferior to him, or to any white person. When the phrenologists came to measure Singbe's head, Lieutenant Meade told them all his personal characteristics: melancholy, murderous, stubborn, insensible. He had them all catalogued — the characteristics of a murderer — and he had no wish to change his mind.

Singbe's first reaction to Lieutenant Meade's order was normal. Meade was the first man to board the *Amistad* and he had treated them roughly. Meade was the friend of the Spaniards. Meade was the friend of Antonio, whom the Africans disliked and distrusted. Meade was the man who had taken such an interest in the gold doubloons that were supposed to be found among the captain's effects. That interest had become common gossip, and when Lewis Tappan publicly accused Lieutenant Meade of stealing the doubloons, the lieutenant opened action for libel against him.

Furthermore, Singbe was growing very cocky, as were the other Africans. Now they knew they would not be charged with piracy or murder. What they did not understand was the degree of jeopardy in which they still lived: the Administration was very much inclined to regard slaves as private property, returnable to their owners. The odds against the African captives being freed in Judge Judson's court were far greater than any reasonable man would care to contemplate.

Lewis Tappan and a crowd of ardent abolitionists constantly hovered around the Negroes, protecting them and demanding comforts in their name. The Africans soon had a good supply of pocket money, which they used to buy sweets and items of amusement. They also used the money to buy rum from Colonel Pendleton's saloon. Consequently, for several days a number of the captives were drunk a good part of each evening, and one night their drunkenness erupted in an orgy of temper that led Colonel Pendleton to subdue the blacks in the best way he knew how — with a whip.

The abolitionists complained — although they had supplied the money for the rum — and it was agreed that the savages were unable to hold their liquor and no more would be sold to them.

Nathaniel Jocelyn, one of the New Haven abolitionists, decided to paint a portrait of Singbe, and the sittings soon began. Jocelyn was not only one of the leading abolitionists in public, he was one of the most dedicated in private: his home was to become a key station on the underground railroad, which spirited escaped Negro slaves from the Southern states into Canada.[3]

The members of the American Anti-Slavery Society were unrelenting in their efforts to free the Africans, and were particularly suspicious of President Van Buren and the Administration. It was, in a way, unfair to take this view: Van Buren was not a slaver; indeed he was of good sturdy New York Dutch stock and he had no interest in slavery personally. But Van Buren's consummate skill as a politician in not taking a stand unless absolutely necessary earned him the enmity of the abolitionists.

During the trial at Hartford the abolitionists became convinced that a better mode of communication with the Africans was essential for the second trial: they had to show oral proof — as they had no documents or physical proof — that the Africans had actually been spirited away from the mouth of the Gallinas River to Havana's Misericordia *barracoon*.

Yale's Professor Gibbs meanwhile was searching New Yorks City's docks and taverns for an interpreter. He marched up and down the wharves, his linguistic papers in hand, and his top hat set firmly on his head. He went from black man to black man, holding up fingers and saying:

"Eta."

"Fili."

"Kiauwa."

"Naeni."

They shook their heads, either laughing or sorrowful to see a white man in such woeful mental condition.

But one day Professor Gibbs' spare figure was promenading on the waterfront, when he encountered a man who informed him that the British cruiser H.M.S. *Buzzard* was in port, having just brought in two prizes — two slave ships that would sail the seas no more.

Professor Gibbs made his way to Quarantine at Staten Island across the harbor, and there he found the *Buzzard*. Aboard he met a young Negro named James Covey, who told him that the words he was saying signified numbers in Mendi, the language of the people who lived just east of the Gallinas River in West Africa. Covey was born at Benderi in the Mendi country, of a Konno father and a Gissi mother. He had been captured as a slave when he was very young and sold into the country of the Bulloms, who lived at their capital of Mani. He lived there for three years and worked in the rice fields; then he was sold to a Portuguese slaver along with 300 other slaves in Mani, and he was taken to Lomboko.

After a month, James Covey was sold to a slaver who intended to take him secretly to America, but after four days out of port the Portuguese slave ship was captured by a British cruiser and taken into Sierra Leone, where the prize was broken up and the slaves declared free men.

This youth, then in his teens, had chosen to remain in Sierra Leone and learn the white man's ways. He had begun learning English at the schools of the Church Missionary Society and had studied there for five years. There his name was changed from the original African Kaweli to the Christian name of James by his teacher, the Reverend J.W. Weeks, of the British missionary society.

In 1838 Captain Fitzgerald had been assigned with the *Buzzard* to patrol the West African station in search of slave ships, and he had put into Sierra Leone, seeking native interpreters to help him discover the facts about the ships he captured. He had gone to the missionary society, and there he had met James Covey, who was persuaded to enlist in the British naval service as interpreter and seaman.

Professor Gibbs climbed the rope ladder from the pilot boat and began talking to young Covey about the Mendi people. He also spoke about the *Amistad* captives, saying he believed they were mostly Mendis. The Professor asked Covey's captain if he might borrow the seaman as an interpreter. Captain Fitzgerald, eager to do anything he could to facilitate the end of another slave ship, agreed to let James Covey go to New Haven for as long as he was needed. Covey and another Mendi-speaking Negro the professor had found on the *Buzzard* left for New Haven with Professor Gibbs.

In the second week of October the professor and his party arrived in New Haven. They went to the prison, but the captives were at breakfast, and Colonel Pendleton was not inclined to let the visitors in until they were finished — he was sick of the abolitionists by this time. But James Covey began speaking Mendi in a loud voice, and then there was no peace for Pendleton until he unlocked the door to the captives' quarters.

Lewis Tappan and his lawyers considered the problems they might face in the coming November resumption of the *Amistad* case in court. First they must hear the full stories of the captives. Then they could act.

For the first time the *Amistad* captives were able to tell their story fluently. They now gave details of their capture and of the trip across the Atlantic on the slave ship. They gave details of the slave *barracoon* at Lomboko. Perhaps if the abolitionists had been able to present such overwhelming testimony at the trial at Hartford, the outcome would have been different, for the denial of the Spaniards that the Negroes were Africans could not hold much weight in court.

On October 7 in New Haven's county court there were filed two briefs, with an eye to bringing charges against the Spaniards. The purpose was to entangle the Spaniards and harry them. The reason was a change in personnel in the Spanish mission in Washington, which had brought a more ambitious and impatient minister to the national capital.

In September Don Añgel Calderon de la Barca had quitted his post as Spanish minister, in favor of the Caballero (Chevalier) Pedro Alcantara Argaiz, on October 3 the Caballero had demanded of Secretary Forsyth a progress report on the return of the *Amistad* and its captives to Spanish hands. Quoting a note from the Spanish consul at Boston, the new minister wrote:

> As it appears from the papers of the schooner that she, as well as her cargo, are exclusively Spanish property, it seems strange that the court of New London has not yet ordered the delivery of one or both to the owners, if they are present, or to me, as their agent, born in that part of the Union, agreeably to the articles of the treaty now in force between the two countries. The delay in the delivery would not be of so much consequence

to the proprietors if the vessel did not require immediate repairs, in order to preserve her from complete destruction, and if it were not material that a large portion of the cargo should be sold on account of its bad conditions.

Argaiz indicated that he expected Secretary Forsyth to see the President and secure speedy determination of all questions pertaining to the *Amistad*.

The letter was enough to make a Secretary of State nervous. It was also enough, when the news leaked out, to warn the abolitionist leaders and the lawyers for the *Amistad* captives that counteraction must be forthcoming.

The only possible counteraction, as the lawyers saw it, was to bring charges against the two Spaniards, who now were represented as owners of the vessel as well as of the cargo, or parts of it. All the cargo that Don Pedro really owned was the four little slaves; and so the objective of the new Spanish minister was quite clear — he was trying his best to secure an administrative judgment by the President of the United States that would hasten or undermine the court's decision.

One of the affidavits filed on October 7 was Singbe's (his name, as usual, was misspelled):

> Singweh, a colored man, deposeth and saith, that he was born at Mani, a town in Jopoa in the Mendi country in Africa, and that his king Mahe Katumbo resided at Kwomendi, the capital of Jopoa in said Mendi country; that he was sold by Birmaja, son of Shaka, king of Genduma in the Fai country, to a Spaniard about six moons ago, that he was brought from Lomboko in a vessel with two masts, that he was landed at a village one day from Havana, where he was kept five days, then he was taken to another village nearer to Havana where he was kept five days more, that he was taken thence by night on foot through Havana to the vessel which brought him from Havana; that he was driven by force and put on board said vessel; that they sailed the next morning, that by night his hands were confined by irons; that

on board said vessel he had not half enough to eat or drink, only two potatoes and one plantain twice a day, and half a tea-cup of water morning and evening; that he was beaten on the head by the cook in the presence of Pipi [Don José] who claims to be his owner, and Montes; and that he was told one morning after breakfast that the white men would eat them when they landed. . . .[4]

Then Fuleh, another *Amistad* captive, swore in another affidavit:

Fuleh, a colored man, deposeth and saith that he was born at Mainu in the Mendi country in Africa, that his king was Tikbah. that he was caught by soldiers and sold to Luis, a Spaniard, at Lomboko; that he was brought to Havana, and landed by night in a small village where he was kept five nights, thence carried to another village where he was kept five nights more; that he was taken through Havana by night and forced on board the vessel which brought him from Havana, and that on board said vessel he had half eat and half drink, that for stealing water which had been refused him he was held down by four sailors and beaten on the back many times by another sailor with a whip having many lashes; that salt, rum, and powder were applied to his wounds; that this flogging was repeated four times on himself, and also on Kimbo, Pie, Moru and Funi, and that all this was done in the presence of Pepe, who bought and claims him, and further that the marks of the wounds are still visible. . . .[5]

These affidavits were the first official words from the *Amistad* captives of their side of the story of the sailing of their ship — and they indicated why the slaves had risen against their captors. But the affidavits were made for an additional purpose: it had been decided that suit would be filed against the Spaniards to fore-stall the shipment of the Africans back to Spanish territory, if the *Amistad* case itself was lost.

That day, James Covey was duly sworn as interpreter and translator, and newspapermen from Boston, Hartford, New

Haven, and New York were treated to the first telling of the full story of the *Amistad* captives.[6]

George Day reported to the New York *Journal of Commerce* that the Africans' story was a very impressive one: "The perfect coincidence in the testimony of the prisoners, examined as they have been separately, is felt by all who are acquainted with the minutes of the examination, to carry with it overwhelming evidence of the truth of their story."

This statement seemed necessary, because throughout the South and wherever there was sympathy for slavery, the first reaction to the *Amistad* story had been that these were simply unruly blacks, slaves of the Spanish, who had decided to run away, had captured their ship, become pirates, and cooked up a tale of fresh capture from Africa to cover their crimes.

All afternoon the captives told their tales; the lawyers had decided it was time the public knew the story of the *Amistad* so that it could be rallied to support the captives in their coming ordeal. Indeed, the opposition of the press was the most formidable faced by the slavers, because in cold print could be told the stories of slaving in all its horrors — in a day when the printed word represented the ultimate in mass communication.

Gilabaru, second in command of the captives, was selected to tell his story for the newspapermen, and it was paraphrased by James Covey:

> On board the vessel [from Africa] there was a large number of men, but the women and children were by far the most numerous. They were fastened together by couples by the wrists and legs and kept in that situation day and night. [Here Gilabaru and Kimbo lay down on the floor to show the painful position in which they were obliged to sleep.] By day it was no better. The space between decks was so small — according to their account not exceeding four feet — that they were obliged, if they attempted to stand, to keep a crouching posture. The decks, fore and aft, were crowded to overflowing. They suffered terribly. They had

rice enough to eat but they had very little to drink. If they left any of the rice that was given to them uneaten, either from sickness or any other cause, they were whipped. It was a common thing for them to be forced to eat so much as to vomit. Many of the men, women and children died on the passage. . .

The intimate details given by the Africans were only hinted at by the sensitive newspaper writers, as when the Spanish gentleman Don José Ruiz made his slave purchases: "Pipi, or Ruiz, selected such as he liked and made them stand in a row. He then felt of each of them in every part of the body; made them open their mouths to see if their teeth were sound, and carried the examination to a degree of minuteness of which only a slave dealer would be guilty."

Gilabaru told of the causes of the rebelloin in a graphic fashion (and it must be remembered that they had not been told to the American public before — the affidavits given that morning had not yet been published). "They were very hungry and suffered much in the hot days and nights from thirst. In addition to this there was much whipping and the cook told them that when they reached land they would all be eaten. This made their hearts burn. To avoid being eaten and to escape the bad treatment they experienced, they rose upon the crew with the design of returning to Africa."

During this session Kimbo was asked how he liked the United States. He liked the country he said, because "they are good people — they believe in God and there is no slavery here."[7]

As the story was translated back to the other Africans, they stood around in a circle, nodding acquiescence and agreement and sometimes adding details for the press. Singbe noted that there was scarcely room to stand or sit during the trip from Africa. Another showed the slave bracelet marks on his wrists. Singbe recalled how they were all in tears at Havana because they were to be parted forever.

As Singbe told this story on October 7 he did not know that there were forces at work to achieve this end even yet, and that every day of delay tended to increase the interest of Americans in the *Amistad* story and to work with the authorities against their release.

10/Diversionary Action

In September, before they went to Hartford to try the first
Amistad case in the Circuit Court, the lawyers Staples and
Sedgwick had addressed a letter to President Van Buren as soon
as they learned that the Spanish authorities were interested
in the *Amistad* captives, and had particularly asked that the
President refrain from interfering in the affair.[1]

The President gathered together the Staples-Sedgwick letter
and the letter from Don Amgel Calderon de la Barca and sent
them to Felix Grundy, Attorney General of the United States,
for an opinion. He did not do this immediately, but waited until
September 24, when the first case had been tried and it was
apparent that the Administration would have to take a definite
position regarding the *Amistad* captives — even if it was only a
hands-off position. President Van Buren apparently did not regard the affair of much significance. There had been cases involving slaves before. Slaves had been returned to their foreign
owners before. There was little reason, on the surface, for
Van Buren to give more than cursory attention to the question
of some forty Negro slaves and a half-wrecked vessel of little
importance.

Attorney General Grundy did not give the matter much thought either, "I have given to the subject all the consideration which its importance demands," he wrote in an undated letter obviously addressed to the Secretary of State "and now present to you, and through you to the President, the result of my reflections upon the whole subject."

He found that the *Amistad* was a Spanish vessel, sailing under legal and regular conditions from Havana, and that the slaves had risen up and killed the captain and taken control of the ship, wandering about the seas until they came to Long Island, where they were siezed. There was no discrepancy between his findings and the facts already revealed.

But what about the ship's papers? To be sure, they were in order, but Staples and Sedgwick had indicated that the slaves could not possibly be what the papers said they were — *ladinos.*

The Attorney General did not wish to consider the facts here. It could do no good, he said: "Besides, in this case, were the Government of the United States to permit itself to go behind the papers of the schooner *Amistad,* it would place itself in the embarrassing condition of judging upon the Spanish laws, their force, effect, and their application to the case under consideration."[2]

He continued: "I cannot see any legal principle upon which the Government of the United States would be authorized to go into an investigation for the purpose of ascertaining whether the facts stated in those papers by the Spanish officers are true or not. Suppose, however, that the evidence contained in these papers should not be entitled to all the effect I have given it; would that change or alter the course which should be pursued by the government?"

No, said Attorney General Grundy, it would not. The government of the United States must consider the Negroes of the *Amistad* to be the property of the Spaniards on whose behalf the Spanish government had made a claim.

Grundy also affirmed the position of the Circuit Court — that there were no grounds on which the Africans might be tried in the United States for piracy or murder.

Then he considered what was to be done with the vessel and the cargo — "the Negroes being a part of the latter." The treaty must be observed. The cargo and vessel must be delivered to the Spanish minister or the person he designated. He went on:

> 1. The owners of the vessel and cargo are not all in this country, and, of course, a delivery cannot be made to them.
>
> 2. This has become a subject of discussion between the two Governments, and in such a case, the restoration should be made to that agent of the Government who is authorized to make and through whom the demand is made.
>
> 3. These Negroes are charged with an infraction of the Spanish laws; therefore it is proper that they should be surrendered to the public functionaries of that Government, that if the laws of Spain have been violated, they may not escape punishment.
>
> 4. These Negroes deny that they are slaves; if they should be delivered to the claimants, no opportunity may be afforded for the assertion of their right to freedom. For these reasons it seems to me that a delivery to the Spanish minister is the only safe course for this Government to pursue.[3]

Perhaps Attorney General Grundy really did believe that if the slaves were returned to the Spanish minister, and he returned them to Havana, the corrupt Captain General of Cuba would deal honestly and honorably with them, admitting his own malfeasance of the past. Grundy *might* have been so naive — but none of the abolitionists believed so.

A search began for Don José Ruiz and Don Pedro Montes, because Secretary of State Forsyth, after reading the letter from the Attorney General, wanted copies of the papers of the *Amistad*. District Attorney Holabird initiated a search to discover where Don José Ruiz and Don Pedro Montes had gone after the first trial was ended and the second was recessed.

The Spaniards were found in New York, not by District Attorney Holabird, but by the representatives of the abolitionists, on October 17 at the Spanish Hotel on Fulton Street.

Lewis Tappan accompanied Deputy Sheriff Joseph Keen to the hotel, where they interrupted Don José and Don Pedro at lunch with the news that they were arrested. They wanted to know why, but the deputy told them only that he had two instructions: to arrest them and to allow them to make arrangements for bail before he took them to jail.

They went to the office of a New York merchant, a Spaniard named Granja, who offered to put up bail. But on advice of one of their counsel, the Spaniards decided to go to jail, hoping to win some sympathy for themselves and hoping also that the noise of their going would be heard in Madrid and in Washington. Abolitionist Tappan abused the Spaniards as slaveholders, and the Spaniards abused him as an interfering busybody, and then the Spaniards were courteously escorted to The Tombs, then the pride of the city because of its unique architecture. The Spaniards were given a comfortable cell on the fourth tier, far above the common herd of drunks and pilferers, where they had overstuffed chairs and good beds, clean linen, pictures on the walls, and the privilege of ordering food and drink from outside whenever they wanted it. They also had the privilege of entertaining visitors.

The Spaniards settled down to a wait in jail. The abolitionists redoubled their efforts to obtain money and support for the cause of the *Amistad* prisoners, and their newspaper was very heavily devoted to this cause in the subsequent weeks.

When word was received in Madrid and in Washington that Señors Ruiz and Montes had been arrested in New York and imprisoned on the complaint of *slaves*, there was indeed an uproar. On October 22 Argaiz wrote a very strong letter of protest to the State Department, asking President Van Buren to intervene, free them and indemnify them for the injuries and losses they may have suffered in the imprisonment.

That letter did not long languish in the files of the official correspondence. Secretary Forsyth could move when he felt so impelled, and after consulting with President Van Buren he replied two days later: It was his painful duty to instruct the Spanish Minister in the ways of the American system, under which the courts were open to all. "The Constitution and laws having secured the judicial power against all interference on the part of the Executive authority, the President, to whom the Chevalier de Argaiz's note has been communicated, has instructed the undersigned to state that the agency of this government to obtain the release of Messrs. Ruiz and Montes cannot be afforded in the manner requested by him."[4]

He did report that the President had asked the United States Attorney in the District of New York, Benjamin F. Butler, to look in on the Spaniards and offer them any advice and assistance that he could legally offer.

In a few days the Spanish government's attorneys called for the release of the two Spaniards by Butler. When Judge Inglis heard the case, he decided that Montes should be released, since he was simply a witness in the assault and battery case brought in behalf of the *Amistad* captives, but that José Ruiz should be kept on $250 bail. Montes went back to the Spanish hotel. Don José chose to remain in jail.

On October 29 Argaiz himself went to New York to see Don José in jail and United States Attorney Butler at the United States Court House. Butler was very affable, but, as he told the minister, there was really nothing he could do because the matter was being carried through the courts of the State of New York, over which the federal government had no direct jurisdiction. Making the representative of an absolute monarchy understand the American system was beyond the United States Attorney's abilities, but he did the best he could, and the Spanish minister was satisfied with the attention he received if not with the answers.

After this visit, the Spanish minister posed a sharp question to the Secretary of State. The Spanish-American Treaty of 1795, he said, provided specifically for the return of property and a specific manner of handling legal cases:

> It is allowed by the whole world that a court cannot take cognizance of crimes or delinquencies committed in other countries, or other jurisdictions, and under other laws, the application of which is not intrusted to it; as, also that petitions or accusations of slaves against their masters cannot be admitted in a court. If, however, this were not all well known and established, does not the seventh article of the treaty of 1795 apply to this case? What says that article? It says that in case an American citizen should contract debts or commit offenses in the dominions of His Catholic Majesty, or a Spaniard in the United States, the proceedings for his arrest and all others against him shall be conducted in a manner already established &c &c.

The Spanish minister cited the case of a sea captain named Wendell, who had been taken into a Spanish court for the mistreatment of his mate, Mr. Bell, on Spanish soil. This case had been handled by the Spanish with despatch and according to the letter of the treaty of 1795. Abraham Wendell, captain of the brig *Franklin*, was treated exactly as was proper under the treaty, and the Spanish government did not attempt to go beyond its treaty rights.

Using this affair as a fulcrum, the Spanish minister asked:

> And as the incompetence of the courts of the United States, with regard to this matter, is so clearly demonstrated, is there no power in the Federal Government to declare it so, and to interpose its authority to put down the irregularity of these proceedings, which the court is not competent to perform? It seems impossible that there should be no such power, but, unfortunately, there is none.

Her Catholic Majesty's envoy extraordinary and minister pleni-
potentiary. . . asks the Secretary of State whether or not he possesses
sufficient authority and force to carry into fulfilment the treaty
of 1795? If he has not, then there can be no treaty binding on
the other party.[5]

That was the statement the Secretary of State and President
Van Buren had been trying desperately to avoid. The actions
of the abolitionists in New England and New York were sorely
trying to the Administration because they interfered with the
normal flow of government and, here, with the normal relationships between sovereign states.

If one was able to ignore the subject matter of the dispute
for a few moments, it would be easy to sympathize with the
position of the Administration. There was a treaty, and it was
specific in its stipulations. The problem arose behind the treaty.
for it was apparent that the Spanish law of Spain and the
enforcement of that law in Cuba were two different matters.
Yet it was not the province of the government of the United
States to tell Her Majesty in Madrid that the wool was being
pulled over her eyes in the matter of slavery in the New World.

Secretly, in answer to pleas for guidance from Holabird and
Ingersoll, Attorney General Grundy composed a letter that was
not revealed to Congress or the public:

> The President, he said, concurs in the opinions expressed by
> the Attorney General and wishes them carried out.
> The course is decided on but it is deemed expedient to make
> no communication of it to anyone until the property is freed from
> all judicial action, he will then act promptly in carrying out the
> opinion of the Attorney General.[6]

So President Van Buren was finally on record — he did not
want it known, but he would turn over the slaves to the Spanish
without a whiffle. Here in the secret books of the Administration

was as close to an admission of the Van Buren policy as the historians were ever to get.

In mid-November the case of the Negroes against the Spaniards was again brought to New York City's courts for hearing before Judge Inglis, and Caballero Argaiz and United States Attorney Butler attended.

Don José spoke in his own defense, his command of English being adequate to the task. He spent much of his time describing the circumstances of the purchase of the slaves and his horrifying two-month voyage as a prisoner. He then attacked the American system, the American abolitionists — Lewis Tappan in particular — for their interference in commerce between nations.

When Don José finished his speech, attorney Sedgwick asked for permission for Tappan to reply. Tappan did reply, saying that he was only trying to help the poor, friendless Africans. If not entirely a candid reply, it was at least very effective in the courtroom that day and made an excellent record for the abolitionists.

It was apparent to Judge Inglis that there was much to be considered, and he laid the case over, hoping for some signs from the courts in Connecticut. Don Pedro was free to leave the country. Don José was free on bail.

A few days later, Don Pedro boarded a schooner for Cuba to escape the never-ending conflict.

11/Judge Judson Presides

The District Court cases involving the *Amistad* captives were opened in the Connecticut State Senate Chamber in Hartford on November 19, with a capacity crowd in attendance. Judge Andrew Judson was presiding, which caused muttering among the abolitionists, who had not forgotten his behavior when Prudence Crandall had welcomed a Negro girl into her school next to the judge's house.

During the recess the air had seemed filled with flying papers. The lawyers had entered motions and countermotions, affidavits, and depositions. In Washington, President Van Buren had decided that the treaty with Spain must be honored and was ready to issue a warrant of extradition, which was one way the executive branch could seek to honor the terms of the treaty. Of course, the Administration realized that if the order was issued it would be contested hotly by the abolitionists, and then it could not help but become a serious political issue for the campaign of 1840.[1] So the President and his advisers decided to wait until the District Court in Connecticut acted. If the court decided to turn the Africans over to the Spanish government, the problem would be off the back of the executive branch.

President Van Buren was watching the case very closely.

During the court recess District Attorney Holabird visited him in Albany, where the President kept his permanent home. They conferred on the various details of the case, and Van Buren authorized Holabird to employ assistant counsel, so complex had the case become because of the interference of many parties.

The district attorney filed a new libel in court, setting out the claim of Spain, and interjecting a new issue. The mulatto cabin boy Antonio wanted to return to Cuba and to slavery, and he petitioned that he be put in the consul's charge to that end. The consul in Boston also had gotten together the claims of the various heirs of Captain Ferrer and other owners of cargo on the *Amistad,* and these claims were submitted to the court. In behalf of the Africans, first a new plea that the court had no jurisdiction was entered; this was supplanted by a plea that they had simply asserted their right to freedom in taking possession of the vessel.

On November 19, when court opened the first matter to be taken up was the claim of Lieutenant Commander Gedney and Lieutenant Meade for salvage.

The naval officers persisted in asking for reward, using the usual forms, which included the statement that they deserved reward for "meritorious service." Such words infuriated the abolitionists and caused them to write contemptuous and sometimes misleading articles in abolitionist journals, like William Cullen Bryant's New York *Evening Post.*

In this case the facts were established, as they had not been in the cases of the hearings before the Circuit Court. The lawyer Roger Baldwin established the conditions of the seizure of the Africans (District Attorney Holabird had investigated and determined that the seizure was conducted on the high seas). The Negroes, said Baldwin, were *Africans.* They were kidnaped and transported to Cuba by persons to them unknown. They had never lived in Cuba, but had immediately been sold to Ruiz and Montes, and taken aboard the *Amistad.* They had risen only to secure their own freedom and had determined to sail the ship back to Africa.

The Africans' counsel contended that the ship had not been a mile offshore, as District Attorney Holabird claimed, but had been less than three-quarters of a mile offshore, at the time of capture. Further, at least twenty of the captives were on the soil of the State of New York at this moment. Consequently, the District Court of Connecticut had no jurisdication at all in this case.

The counsel for Lieutenant Commander Gedney and Lieutenant Meade objected to the interjection of the *Amistad* captives' attorneys into the case, but Baldwin said that the rights and even perhaps the lives of the Negroes were at stake, for if the claims of the naval men were allowed, then the Africans would be declared the property of the Spaniards and would have to go back to Havana.[2]

The counsel for Gedney and Meade said no — he did not wish the court to prejudge or judge in this matter the position of the Africans, but simply the rights or wrongs of the claims of the naval men against the Spaniards. Judge Judson then allowed counsel for the Africans to participate in the first part of the action.

Six of the Africans appeared in court during this procedure; the rest were left behind in New Haven. Señor Vega, the vice-consul of Spain from Boston, sat at one table. The counsel for Don José Ruiz was there, to join the counsel for Lieutenant Commander Gedney, and Governor Ellsworth, counsel for Captain Green of Long Island, who still hoped to achieve something by his claim for salvage.

The case was delayed, confused, and rendered nearly impossible by the illness of James Covey, who had stayed in New Haven. Thus, when Captain Green declared that the schooner *Amistad* was no farther than 30 rods offshore when captured and District Attorney Holabird declared it was a mile offshore, the Africans could not be successfully questioned to get the truth.

During the early part of the hearing, Holabird suggested that Judge Judson order the vessel, cargo, and slaves to be disposed of in a manner that would comply with the United States obligation to Spain under the treaty of 1795. This action, of course, was what President Van Buren wanted; from his position, the entire *Amistad* affair was simply an unnecessary embarrassment that played into the hands of his political enemies.

Baldwin asked for a postponement until James Covey recovered and was able to interpret the testimony of the Africans. He might or might not have won the postponement on its merits, but Isham, who represented the naval officers, was called home on an emergency, and Judge Judson decided that it would be proper to grant a postponement of the case until the next meeting of the District Court, which was scheduled for New Haven on January 7, 1840.

This delay was agreeable to the *Amistad* captives' attorneys, with one exception, which was to prove major in the case.

Lewis Tappan had become one of the most famous — or infamous — men in America because of the *Amistad* case. He had been in touch with Dr. Richard Robert Madden, a British resident of Havana who served in various official capacities with the Mixed Commission that adjudicated slave-ship cases. At the time of the *Amistad* trial Madden held the position of Superintendent of Liberated Africans. He had earlier been the Resident British Commissioner on the Mixed Commission.

Dr. Madden was persuaded to come to the United States to testify in the trial because Tappan convinced him of the extreme importance of the *Amistad* case to the suppression of slave trade everywhere.

When Dr. Madden arrived in New York he went immediately to Tappan's office to discuss the *Amistad* affair. The delay in the trial created a problem for Dr. Madden, because he had government business to attend to and could not remain indefinitely. But he did take the time to go to New Haven to interview the Africans, in the presence of James Covey, and then to Hartford to appear at the court. The difficulty was resolved on the afternoon of November 20, when Judge Judson allowed Dr. Madden to testify by deposition.

Dr. Madden identified himself as a British official with the Mixed Commission and told of his experience. He had also served in Sierra Leone and was completely familiar with all aspects of slave trade, and with Africa and Africans.

He said he had visited the African prisoners from the *Amistad* at New Haven, with the exception of the children, and he had observed their appéarance, manner, and language. There was no doubt at all that these men were *bozales* — Negroes recently imported from Africa.

He had tested one of them by reciting a Moslem prayer in Arabic, and the African had recognized it. The African had recognized the words "Allah akbar" (God is great), and had repeated some of the words of the Arabic prayer.

Dr. Madden then turned to another Negro. "Salaam aleichem," he said. ("Peace be on you.")

"Aleichem salaam," replied the Negro courteously. ("On you be peace.")

Dr. Madden was shown the license, or *traspasso*, which had permitted the 49 Negroes to be taken from Havana to Puerto Principe aboard the *Amistad*. He noted that on the license the Negroes were called *ladinos*. Here he corrected the error in translation that had been made by the American officials. *Ladinos*, he said, did not mean "sound" or "able-bodied," as the translators had until this point been assuming. *Ladinos* referred specifically to Negroes in Cuba who were resident there *prior to the Spanish treaty with England of 1820*. It had been agreed in that year that *no more* Negroes would be imported into Spanish possessions as slaves. Because slavery was still recognized as legal and although new slave trading was not legal, this distinction was most important.

Dr. Madden was certain that the *Amistad* Negroes were all *bozales*, except perhaps Antonio, who might or might not have been brought into Cuba just at the time of the treaty.

Roger Baldwin also produced the license of Don Pedro Mendes, which permitted him to take there Negro children from Havana to Puerto Principe. Baldwin noted that the children, too, were referred to as *ladinos,* and he said that that was physically impossible.

Dr. Madden was then questioned by his friendly interlocutors as the customs of the illegal slave traders in Cuba. He said he knew that slaves were landed illegally, night after night, and taken to the *barracoons.* There the *bozales* were kept for two or three weeks until sold. Also, he said that one of the most notorious of the slave-trading houses in Cuba was Martinez and Company, whose representatives had signed the transfer of the children to Don Pedro.

On September 24, after he had been in touch with Lewis Tappan, Dr. Madden had visited the Misericordia *barracoon* in Havana. By that time the story of the *Amistad* was well known in Havana. In conversation with Señor Riera and his major-domo, Dr. Madden had come to the subject of the *Amistad* and its human cargo.

Yes, the major-domo and Señor Riera remembered the *Amistad* captives well. They had been in the *barracoon,* and they had been purchased by a young man who intended to take them to Puerto Principe. What a pity it was, said the slave dealers, that these slaves had been allowed to escape and cause so much trouble. What an unfortunate loss! (The two slave dealers assumed, on the basis of their experience in the trade in Cuba, that the slaves would be executed in the United States for piracy and murder.)

Dr. Madden also testified as to the procedure a man followed when he wished to transfer a slave from one point in the Cuban isles to another. He would go to the Havana, the government house, and apply to the authorities for a permit. Although the procedure was simple, it involved paying a head tax of $10 to $15 to secure the Governor General's signature on the document. There was never any trouble if the head tax was paid, nor did the Governor General or any of his officials ever question an application or investigate the status of the Negroes in transit.

Thus a *bozal* became a *ladino* simply by the Governor General's declaration that this was so — and the applicant need not even sign an oath that the Negroes were long-time residents of Cuba and not illegally imported new slaves.

Dr. Madden pointed out, under careful questioning, that the misrepresentation of the status of the Negroes was a fraud on the part of the purchaser, that it was part of the connivance at the illegal slave trade, and that there was obvious collusion between the authorities and the slave traders every day. Thousands of *bozales* were still being imported into Cuba, although under Spanish law no Negro who was imported after the year 1820 was *legally enslaved.*

The Spanish authorities in Cuba were so self-contained and so heedless of the wishes of their sovereign that they had no need to make a distinction between *ladinos* and *bozales.* The distinction was made, and the papers were carefully fabricated on each slave transfer, for the simple purpose of foiling the British and other slave cruisers off the coast of Cuba. Slave cruising — the arrest and capture of slavers — was a bountiful occupation in these years for adventurous captains. Some naval officers were assigned to the work and many volunteered because the British Crown paid a bounty of five guineas for every slave illegally captured who was released after trial before a Mixed Commission. A "catch" of 400 slaves would yield the slave-catchers' captain 2,000 guineas, a very handsome sum.

The lawyers for the *Amistad* captives returned to their central point, for which they had elicited Dr. Madden's expert testimony. He was, at the time of his testimony, in charge of the affairs of hundreds of *bozal* Negroes in and around Havana who were being moved — either back to Africa or to some other free territory such as the British West Indies. He was in a position to know the ages of the captives, and he stated that the youngest of them, Sa, was about seventeen, which would have made it physically impossible for him to be a *ladino.*

By this time it was apparent that District Attorney Holabird

was following the dictates of the Van Buren Administration, and
that the Administration was seeking the return of the *Amistad*
captives, the physical cargo, and the ship to the Spanish minister
so that the case might be rapidly closed. Before this day Holabird
had appeared in one guise, that of defender of law and order;
on November 20 he appeared as the ardent prosecutor, and it
was in this attitude that he approached the cross-examination
of Dr. Madden in the courtroom, doing his best to disqualify
the Englishman as an expert witness. The questions and answers
went as follows:

Q. Are you acquainted with the language of any African nation
or tribe?

A. I am not acquainted with the dialects of the African tribes,
but am slightly acquainted with the Arabic, and in those parts
of Africa where Mahommedanism prevails, the principal forms
of prayer are repeated in that language.

Q. Are not lawful slaves in Cuba, when offered for sale, often
or generally placed in the *barracoons?*

A. They are not.

Q. Are not lawful slaves in any part of the island placed in
the *barracoons?*

A. At Havana they are not. I cannot say what is done elsewhere, but on whatever part of the coast the slave trade is
carried on there must be *barracoons;* they are things that belong
to it, and are used exclusively for it. When Creole slaves are sold
in this country they are sold on the estates or with them.

Q. Is not the use of the native languages often continued for a
long time on certain plantations?

A. I should say the very reverse of this was the fact. It has
been a matter of astonishment to me to observe the shortness of
the time in which their native language is disused by the African
Negroes, and the Spanish language adopted and acquired.

Q. Was not the limit of your duties at Havana; and therefore
the circumstances alluded to may not have been within your
knowledge?

A. On the subject of slavery in Cuba, and of the condition of the Negroes held in slavery, I believe I am as fully informed as any foreigner can be; I have visited a great many estates and made many journeys into the interior.

Q. How many *barracoons* are there at Havana and how many in other parts of the island?

A. There are five or six at Havana, outside the walls and contiguous to the Governor's country house. Wherever the slave trade is carried on they must be established for its use. For instance, in the vicinity of Matanzas there is one, and others on other parts of the coast.

Q. After the Negroes are landed are they not bona fide transferred by sale, without any interference of the Spanish authorities or of the Mixed Commission?

A. When Negroes are introduced at all from Africa into the island of Cuba, they are illegally captured and illegally enslaved. And it unfortunately happens that the Spanish authorities, receiving an impost of $10 per head on each Negro thus introduced, which is called a voluntary contribution but is in reality a tax, which has no legal sanction for its imposition, never interfere to stop this contraband trade and transfer, but connive at it, and collude with the slave traders; the manifest evidence of which is the number of illegal introductions having been, for the last three years, from twenty to twenty-five thousand a year into the island of Cuba. As to the interference of the commission, once the Negroes have been landed, it is not to be looked for; their jurisdiction extends only to cases in violation of the treaty, brought before them by captors of slave ships, but the cognizance of all transgressions of the Spanish law on Spanish soil, in this as in every other case of crime, belongs to the captain general.[3]

Thus ended the cross-examination. District Attorney Holabird objected to the introduction of some of Dr. Madden's remarks, but agreed to let them stand on the understanding that when the trial was resumed in January the entire deposition could be brought into question.[4]

12/The Trial Continues

During the second recess the lawyers and statesmen were very busy indeed, trying to assure victory for themselves. The Spanish minister sensed his growing strength and indicated it in a letter to Secretary of State Forsyth, written in Washington on November 26.[1] He had, for a time, become very impatient, but in November he began to understand that the Administration was doing everything that could be done, in a ticklish political and legal situation, to abide by the terms of the Spanish-American Treaty of 1795. He also had begun to understand how unpopular that treaty — or any treaty that guaranteed the rights of men in other men as slaves — was becoming in the states north of the Mason-Dixon line.[2]

In November, sensing these changes, the Caballero de Argaiz began talking tough. He might have expected the treaty of 1795 to be honored immediately after the *Amistad* was taken to New London.

> Very different, however, have been the results; for in the first place the treaty of 1795 has not been executed, as the legation of Her Catholic Majesty has solicited; and the public vengeance has not been satisfied, for be it recollected that the legation of Spain does not demand the delivery of slaves but of assassins. Secondly,

great injury has been done to the owners; not the least being the imprisonment which Don José Ruiz is now undergoing, notwithstanding the complaints made on that subject, which, if not entirely disregarded, have at least not produced the favorable results which might have been expected; and the dignity of the Spanish nation has thus been offended. With respect to which injuries, the indemnification can fully recomense for the evils, physical and moral, which the persecutions and vexations occasioned by fanaticism may cause to an honorable man.[3]

The Spanish minister struck again, on November 29, against the imprisonment of Don José Ruiz:

The whole nation knows the prosecution has been set on foot legally by three men, who by their declaration that they had been sold in Africa, prove the state of slavery in which they were in that country. Now, if they were slaves in their own country, how do they come to be here in the enjoyment of civil rights? Moreover, a criminal accusation is now hanging over them; and in every civilized country the said rights would be always suspended with respect to persons lying under such accusations.[4]

The Caballero's definition of "civilized country" might be open to question in the United States and the rest of the English-speaking world, but his impatience was unquestionable. It was also unquestionable that he knew by the end of November that the Administration was very favorable to his point of view and was doing all possible to further it. The Van Buren cabinet was willing to issue a warrant of extradition for the Negroes of the *Amistad*. The warrant was delayed for reasons of timing; Van Buren did not wish to make any more of a political issue of the case than necessary.[5]

"As to the delay which already has attended, and still may attend, a final decision, and which the Chevalier de Argaiz considers as a legitimate subject of complaint," wrote Secretary Forsyth on December 12, "it arises from causes which the under-

signed believes it would serve no useful purpose to discuss at
this time, further than to say that they are beyond the control
of this department, and that it is not apprehended that they will
affect the course which the government of the United States
may think it fit ultimately to adopt."[6]

He explained that Don José was in jail because he wanted to
be in jail — all he had to do was post appearance bond. There
was no question in his mind, said the Secretary of State, but
that the case filed against Don José would be settled favorably
to the Spaniard, and that "if the proceedings against Mr. Ruiz
shall be found to have been unwarranted by the existing law,
all the meddling persons who can be shown to have been parties
to his imprisonment are answerable to him. . . . "[7]

The Secretary closed the letter with his assurances that the
government believed the Spaniards to be the aggrieved parties
and that their claim to the surrender of the slaves "was founded
in fact and in justice."

It was the strongest declaration of policy the Administration
had made.

In his reply, the Caballero made one telling point, from the
position of the Spaniards attempting to enforce a treaty. He
wrote to Secretary Forsyth on Christmas Day:

> Possibly the undersigned may not have formed such an accurate
> conception of this affair, since it has been carried within the
> circle of legal subtleties, as he has not pursued the profession
> of the law; but he is well persuaded that, if the crew of the *Amistad*
> had been composed of white men, the court, or the corporation to
> which the government of the Union might have submitted the ex-
> amination of the question, would have observed the rules by which
> it should be conducted under the constitutional institutions of the
> country, and would have limited itself to the ascertainment of
> the facts of the murders committed on the 30th of June; and the
> undersigned does not comprehend the privilege enjoyed by Negroes,
> in favor of whom an interminable suit is commenced in which

everything is deposed by every person who pleases; and, for that object, an English doctor, who accuses the Spanish government of not complying with its treaties, and calumniates the Captain General of the island of Cuba by charging him with bribery. . . .[8]

The charge of bribery and corruption refers to the one made by Dr. Madden in his testimony by deposition before the District Court in Hartford, and as far as dealings between the executive branches of the two governments were concerned, to make such charge would invite a break in relations. The situation had become most delicate and most difficult for all concerned, so much so that Secretary Forsyth arranged a personal interview with the Spanish minister, to convey by means other than formal writings the sympathies of the Administration.

In the privacy of his office at the State Department, Secretary Forsyth reviewed the case with the Spanish minister, and told him he believed the District Court at New Haven would find itself incompetent to deal with the problems of the *Amistad* captives. In that event, he said, making the statement every bit as significant as he could by indirection, it would be best for the Spanish government to be prepared to take immediate charge of the *Amistad*, its cargo and the Negro captives.

The Spanish minister considered this conversation for several hours afterwards, and on December 30 wrote another letter to the Secretary, explaining that the *Amistad* was in no condition to sail, even if she had a crew, which she did not; and that it would be nearly impossible to find an American merchant ship that would take the Africans back to Cuba to stand trial to discover whether or not they were slaves or criminals or both. He asked for the use of an American government ship to send the *Amistad* captives to Cuba, if the court were to free the Africans as not being under its jurisdiction.

On January 5, a few hours before the court was to convene in New Haven, the Secretary told the Spanish minister that President Van Buren had agreed to hold a vessel in readiness for the immediate transfer of the Africans if the court freed them. The Negroes would then be delivered to the Captain General of Cuba. Further he would have a record prepared of all the proceedings in the United States, and Lieutenant Commander Gedney and Lieutenant Meade would be sent to Cuba to testify in the court case to be held there.

In December and early January, events seemed to be moving steadily toward the return of the *Amistad* Africans to Havana, where there was little doubt that they would be adjudged slaves, murderers, and pirates, and be quickly put to death as horrible examples for all other Negroes.

Yet there were certain forces moving for the Negroes at this time as well. The British government had learned of the increasing desire of the Americans to serve the Spanish under the treaty of 1795, and on January 5 the British minister at Madrid wrote to the foreign minister of the Spanish court, saying that he had been instructed "to call upon the government of Her Catholic Majesty to issue with as little delay as possible, strict orders to the authorities of Cuba, that if the request of the Spanish minister at Washington was complied with, these Negroes may be put in possession of the liberty of which they were deprived, and to the recovery of which they have an undeniable title."[9]

Further, the British minister demanded that the laws of Spain against the slave trade be enforced against Don José Ruiz and Don Pedro Mendes for buying Negroes they knew to have been recently imported illegally from Africa.

This weight of British official opinion was not an inconsiderable force in the matter of the *Amistad* captives.

Another force was John Quincy Adams, sixth President of the United States and in 1839 a member of the House of Representatives serving his native Massachusetts. He had first been consulted on the case after the negative decisions on the habeas corpus pleas, back in September. He had grown more interested in the case, and by October 1 he wrote in his diary that it

"now absorbs a great deal of my time and all my good feelings."[10]
In the fall, John Quincy Adams had joined the defenders of the
Amistad captives, although his was still largely an advisory role
and he did not plan to appear in court in New Haven on the
day the trial began again.

He made several points in public letters on the case. On November 19, he wrote from Quincy, Massachusetts to the New
York *Journal of Commerce* to explain his understanding of the
laws of the United States regarding the *Amistad* captives, speaking with the authority of one of the architects of the Treaty of
Ghent, which ended the War of 1812, and had some bearing
on the question of the slaves. The letter said:

> The Africans of the *Amistad* were cast upon our coast in a con-
> dition perhaps as calamitous as could befall human beings, not
> by their own will — not with any intention hostile or predatory on
> their part, not even by the act of God as in the case of ship-
> wreck, but by their own ignorance of navigation and the decep-
> tion of one of their oppressors whom they had overpowered, and
> whose life they had spared to enable them by his knowledge of
> navigation to reach their native land.
>
> They were victims of the African slave trade, recently im-
> ported into the island of Cuba, in gross violation of the laws of
> the Island and of Spain; and by acts which our own laws have
> made piracy — punishable with death. They had indicated their
> natural right to liberty, by conspiracy, insurrection, homicide and
> capture and they were accused by the two Cuban Spaniards em-
> barked with them in the ship, of murder and piracy — and they
> were claimed by the same two Cuban Spaniards, accessories after
> the fact to the slave-trade piracy, by which they had been brought
> from Africa to Cuba, as their property, because they had bought
> them from the slave-trade pirates.
>
> They knew nothing of the Constitution, laws or language of
> the country upon which they were thus thrown, and accused as
> pirates and murderers, claimed as slaves of the very men who
> were then their captives, they were deprived even of the faculty
> of speech in their own defense. This condition was sorely calami-

tous; it claimed from the humanity of a civilized nation *compassion;*
— it claimed from the brotherly love of a Christian land *sympathy;*
— it claimed from a Republic professing reverence for the rights
of man *justice* — and what have we done?

A naval officer of the United States seizes them, their ship and
cargo, with themselves; tramples on the territorial jurisdiction of
the State of New York, by seizing, disarming and sending on board
their ship, without warrant of arrest, several of them whom he
found on shore; releases their captives; admits the claim of the
two captives to fifty masters as their slaves; and claims salvage
for restoring them to servitude. They are then brought before a
court of the United States, at once upon the charge of piracy and
murder, upon a claim to them as slaves, and upon a claim against
their pretended masters for salvage, by kidnaping them again
into slavery. The Circuit Judge decides that the United States
do not exercise the right of all other civilized nations to try piracies
committed in foreign vessels; that he thereupon cannot try them for
piracy or murder, but that the District Court may try whether
they are slaves or not; as it is doubtful whether this trial will be
held in Connecticut or New York, and it must take time to ascertain in which, they shall in the mean time be held as slaves
to abide the issue.

Is this *compassion?* Is it *sympathy?* Is it *justice?* But here the
case now stands.[11]

In another letter,[12] John Quincy Adams offered his services
to the counsel for the defense of the *Amistad* captives, and the
offer was quickly accepted, although it was agreed that he still
would not appear in New Haven. The authority of his name,
the power of his force for liberty in these years was as strong
as that of any man in the nation, and far stronger than the
similar power of the Administration, for no matter what else
was thought about Martin Van Buren, he did not make his mark
as a civil libertarian.

While their cause was arousing so much attention in New
York, Washington, Havana, Madrid, London, and Quincy, Massachusetts the *Amistad* captives remained confined in the New

Haven jail, beginning their first New England winter. Their
friends the abolitionists could do nothing to protect them from
the winds that whipped through the drafty jail, except to provide flannel clothing and plenty of blankets, but they could try
to assist the captives in other ways.

The news that several of the *Amistad* captives were at least
nominally Mohammedans shocked the God-fearing abolitionists
mightily. Lewis Tappan was a warden of his church, and nearly
all the abolitionists, citizens and divines, were very active in
sects of the Protestant religion. They decided that the *Amistad*
captives must not only be taught to read and write but must
also be given religious instruction to preserve them from utter
damnation at some future hour. George E. Day, an instructor
in Hebrew at Yale Divinity School, volunteered to teach the
captives both, now that he had the services of James Covey.[13]

Between studies, Singbe was transported back and forth to
the studio of artist Jocelyn, brother of the Reverend Simeon
Jocelyn, who was one of the original members of the *Amistad*
captives aid committee. Robert Purvis of Charleston, South Carolina, one of the founding fathers of the American Anti-Slavery
Society, had also commissioned a portrait of Singbe. Other paint-
ings and drawings were made, including a hair-raising woodcut
entitled "The Death of Capt. Ferrer, Captain of the *Amistad,*
July, 1839," which showed four Africans mutilating a white man
with cane knives, while another terrified white fled along the
deck, and half-dozen other Africans watched the bloody scene.[14]

The *Amistad* captives threatened to become thoroughly
spoiled, as children are spoiled — there was no question about
that. And yet their situation was anything but childlike, for they
faced slavery and death, and there could be no question about
it at the end of December, 1839. The word of the Administration's attitudes and actions in relation to the captives had
come to New Haven, and the abolitionists were thoroughly frightened in behalf of their charges and thoroughly insistent that
they must not be delivered back into the hands of the Spaniards.

The Africans studied the New Testament and learned hymns, while the abolitionists plotted. They were prepared to break every law of the land to save the Africans. A constant watch was kept on the jail, on the harbor, and on the officials who might spirit the Africans away some dark night. A route was planned to take them to Canada. This plan was in the hands of Lewis Tappan and his brother Arthur.[15]

Arthur was head of the American Colonization Society, an organization founded in the hope that the African slaves in the United States could be returned to Africa to set up their own American-style republics. Liberia was to be the example, but only the example. Arthur Tappan had defended Prudence Crandall in the case in which Judge Judson was involved; he had sent a representative to the Western Reserve to establish Oberlin College as an anti-slavery institution, pledging as much of his annual income of $100,000 to the task as was necessary; he had paid William Lloyd Garrison's fines when he was imprisoned in Philadelphia; he had subsidized scores of anti-slavery tracts and pamphlets.

Now Arthur Tappan and his brother Lewis provided most of the money for the continuation of the defense of the *Amistad* Africans, and they also made the preparations for escape, if such was necessary. They provided a ship, manned it, and provisioned it, and made it ready in New Haven harbor for a speedy departure. If by no other means, the friends of the *Amistad* captives would spirit them away in the dead of night and send them back to Africa illegally.

This decision resulted from the events of January 2, 1840. The State Department sent a letter to the Navy Department, ordering a ship in secret, to be anchored off New Haven not later than January 10 and to "convey the Negroes of the *Amistad* to Cuba." Lieutenant Commander Gedney and Lieutenant Meade were to go along to appear as witnesses at the coming trials of the Negroes in Havana.

The message was delivered by hand. That same day Secretary of the Navy Paulding replied that the United States schooner *Grampus* had been detailed to the task, and that Gedney and Meade would be aboard. The ship would arrive a few days before January 10.[16]

Gedney and Meade were unwise enough to let it be known among their own circle that they were going South to testify in the case of the Africans, and soon the members of the Anti-Slavery Society knew it, too. The alert in New Haven harbor was doubled.

The trial began again on the morning of January 7, 1840, across the New Haven green from the county jail, in the court room of the stately building called the State House. The room was jammed with visitors, who came from as far away as Washington and Boston for the occasion, and the crowd was such that men were arguing about standing room, for the ladies had most of the seats.

The first few hours of the trial were taken up with the necessary dull legal argument. The counsel for the Africans accepted the jurisdiction of the District Court, having denied it in petitions earlier. The room was filled with lawyers, both real and incipient; the real were the counsel for the Africans (three) for Lieutenant Commander Gedney (two), for Captain Green of Long Island (one), for the Spaniards (one), and for the United States government (one). The incipient were the students of Yale Law School, who were relieved of classes during the trial so that they could study this famous case.

After the technical questions were settled in the morning, the first testimony regarding the Africans and their condition was given in the courtroom. James Covey, the interpreter, Professor Gibbs of Yale, and several others were called to testify as to their belief about the length of time the Africans had been away from their native land. All testified that in their opinions the Africans were very newly arrived in the Western Hemisphere.

This evidence continued in the afternoon, and Dr. Madden's deposition was placed in the trial record.

On Wednesday, January 8, the second day of the trial began

with Professor Gibbs being recalled to the witness stand to lend detail to the question of the nationality of the captives.

He began to respond to questioning about the Mendi language and the relationship of the prisoners, most of whom spoke Mendi. He was moving into a technical discussion when Judge Judson interrupted to remark that he was already quite convinced that the *Amistad* captives had recently come from Africa and that it was not necessary to take further time to establish that fact.

The judge's admission was the first victory the Africans had scored in court.

Singbe was called as a witness, to try to determine who and how many were on shore in New York State when they were captured by the United States naval brig *Washington*.

Singbe named about ten others, but said he could not remember exactly how many Africans were ashore that day. Singbe recalled giving Captain Green two guns, a knife, and a hat, and telling the captain that he could have the *Amistad* for his own if he would take them to Sierra Leone.

He was cross-examined by Isham, the attorney for Captain Green. He told how he and several of the others had found the money that belonged to Captain Ferrer and had tied it into cloths they wore around their waists. And what happened to the money? Singbe said he had "given it to the men in the boat," which meant the American sailors under Lieutenant Meade.

The rest of his testimony concerned the trip to and from Cuba, and many of the details he gave were thus made public for the first time. He, Singbe, had been beaten once, by the mulatto cook who hit him with a plantain.

Several other Africans testified that day, Gilabaru and Fuliwa among them. They corroborated Singbe's story and added to it. They said Captain Ferrer had managed to kill one of the Africans, Duevi. The mulatto cook was the first one killed, slain by Singbe.

Much time was spent in attempting to clear up confusion as to whether Singbe was himself a slaver. United States Marshal Wilcox testified that Singbe had indicated that he himself had held slaves and captured slaves in Africa. Through James Covey's interpreting, however. it was established that Wilcox had misunderstood Singbe's early statements, made before there was adequate translation of the Mendi language into English.

The unraveling of this minor mystery consumed all the remaining time in court on Wednesday.

On the third day, Thursday, January 9, various witnesses came forth to testify to their parts in the story. Antonio, the cabin boy slave, testified that Singbe had been the leader of the uprising against the captain and the crew. A deposition from two United States sailors of the *Washington* was introduced to describe the capture of the Africans. The papers of the *Amistad* and of Don José and Don Pedro were introduced as evidence. A witness named D. Francis Bacon was introduced, to testify from personal knowledge of the slave trade at Lomboko and the details of Don Pedro Blanco's trading activities.

On Friday a statement from Spanish Vice-Consul Vega of Boston was introduced, to counteract the deposition of Dr. Madden. Vega said he knew of no law against introducing slaves into Cuba. He said the native languages were often continued in use for years on plantations in Cuba. He said the papers of the *Amistad* and the slave-owners were genuine. (There was no question about that — the question raised was whether the entire transaction, including the Governor General's part, was not fraudulent and illegal.)

But another witness was sworn, who testified that he had called on Señor Vaga in Boston and that the consul had told him that the slave trade in Cuba *was* illegal. Here the implication of señor Vega was mercifully veiled by the court's ending the testimony.

The counsel for the naval officers began their argument to obtain salvage of the ship and its cargo, animate and inanimate.

He contended that the court could not set the Africans free, that whether or not they were delivered to the Spanish authorities or to the United States government, his clients had performed "meritorious services" and deserved to be rewarded.

Governor Ellsworth, counsel for Captain Green, came forward to say that in good conscience he could not ask that the Africans be delivered to the Spanish or United States governments. But if they were to be so delivered, his client must have a part of the salvage money. He contended that Captain Green had rendered the most valuable service, by calming the Africans and persuading them that they were on friendly soil; therefore, the captain and his associates deserved the salvage money more than Lieutenant Commander Gedney and Lieutenant Meade.

Then came lawyers for the various shippers of Havana who had goods aboard the *Amistad*. They argued against any right of salvage to anyone. Lieutenant Commander Gedney had been in the service of his country and was bound to do his duty, so he had no right to claim salvage. Captain Green had not salvaged anything, but had merely attempted to save the *Amistad*. Salvage was to be paid for saving, not for trying to save.

So the case proceeded in orderly fashion.

On Friday afternoon came the opening of argument about the legal status of the Africans. Lawyer Sedgwick led off, followed by Staples, with Roger Baldwin saving his thunder until last.

The Africans in the courtroom were born free, Baldwin said, and they were entitled to their freedom. Those carrying the case against the Africans — including the United States government — maintained that the Africans were slaves and produced licenses. But the licenses were patently fraudulent, the laws of Spain forbade the slave trade, and the captives were not bound by any obedience to Spanish laws. They were not slaves when captured on Long Island and could not be made slaves thereafter.

Baldwin spoke very strongly, denouncing the Spanish minister's interference in the affair as "an insult to the government," and he closed the arguments of the day.

On Saturday, Isham made the closing argument. He said that his clients had authorized him to say that they would never take any salvage on *human flesh*, that all they wanted was that if the court decided the vessel, cargo, and slaves should be restored to the Spaniards, they should be paid reasonable compensation for having restored the Spaniards' property.[17]

The court was recessed for the weekend, and Judge Judson went home to consider what he would do about this strange case — as two low, dark hulls lay out in the water off New Haven, one the *Grampus*, waiting impatiently to take the Africans to Cuba to restore them as slaves and property, and the other the nameless schooner of the Anti-Slavery Society, waiting in case it was called for, with a hundred men ready to help spirit the Africans away from the jurisdiction of all American courts, and far, far from Spain and her tentacles.

13/The Verdict

On the morning of Monday, January 13, 1840, Judge Judson returned to the courtroom, having worked long and hard over the weekend to prepare his lengthy decision in the case of the *Amistad* and its captives. When court opened, he read his decision to the interested parties.

He stated the facts, the progression of events since August 26, when Lieutenant Commander Gedney brought the *Amistad* into New London.

"In the discussion of this case," the judge said, "have been involved numerous questions of great importance, requiring, as we have seen, industrious examination and patient deliberation. It has been my endeavor to afford ample time for this investigation; and the ability with which these questions have been discussed at the bar must satisfy all that everything which talent and learning could accomplish has been done."[1]

The judge was well aware of the international importance of this case: "The case is now only important to those immediately interested, but there are involved principles important to the nation and the world," he said.[2]

First he considered the question of jurisdiction. The *Amistad* was taken in three-and-a-half fathoms of water, not less than half a mile from the shore off Culloden point, five or six

miles from Montauk, about twenty-five miles from Sag Harbor
and eighteen miles from New London. She did not lie in any
known harbor, bay, river, or port. There was scarcely an in-
dentation in the coastline there, and for legal purposes the
schooner was on the high seas when she was seized.

He cited a number of references, and then said that he had
established beyond his own doubt the jurisdiction of the court
and could proceed to consider the legal case on its merits.

Then he considered the claim of Lieutenant Commander
Gedney and Lieutenant Meade against the *Amistad* and its
goods, and separately, against the Africans who were alleged
to be the slaves of Señor Ruiz and Señor Montes.

"First," said the judge, "the claims to salvage for the vessel
and the goods stands upon ground almost beyond question. The
services rendered by Lieutenant Gedney were not only meritorious, but highly praiseworthy. They were such as would entitle
the seizer to his proper allowance. The vessel was at the mercy
of the winds and the waves. She was in the possession and under
the command of these Negroes, who were utterly ignorant
of the science of navigation — without law or order — without
commission or any lawful authority, guided alone by their
ignorance and caprice — just on the point of sailing for the
coast of Africa, and yet without the possibility of conducting
the vessel in safety for a single day."[3]

He considered the objections of the Spanish government,
acting in behalf of Ruiz and Montes, who had not appeared
at this late date. He considered the Spanish government's raising
of the questions in the treaty of 1795, but held that salvage in
this case was reasonable, and ordered an appraisal on the ship
and goods, with a salvage value of one-third of the total to go
to the officers of the *Washington*.

As to the slaves, Judge Judson said, there was no law in
American jurisprudence that would justify the payment of salvage
upon them. How, for example, would a value on the slaves
be placed? It would have to be placed by an appraisal. And who
would appraise?

More important, would they be estimated or appraised by their value in the District of Connecticut? There the value of a slave was absolutely nothing. But could the slaves be valued on the basis of their worth in other states or other countries? Not at all, said the judge, because a court could not hand down a decree that it could not enforce. Thus there was no value in the slaves to be collected.

As to the claims of Captain Henry Green and Pelatiah Fordham, the judge rejected them. Captain Green and Fordham had sold the *Amistad* captives two dogs for a doubloon apiece, and had promised them to be there the next morning. The Americans had planned to take the vessel, but the Africans did not understand that; they expected to be taken to West Africa.

The judge then came to the important questions before him, the questions that concerned the lives and freedom of more than forty men.

Should the Africans be delivered to the Spanish government? If not, what should be done with them?

Having examined the evidence, having listened to all the claims, the judge found that there were three classes of Negroes in Cuba: *creoles,* born in Cuba; *ladinos,* residents since before 1820, and *bozales,* those recently imported from Africa.

He found the *Amistad* Negroes to be *bozales.*

The judge then considered the treaty of 1795 and the claims about the Negroes pertaining to it. The treaty, he said, must be subject to the laws of Spain, and the laws of Spain did not hold that *bozales* could be legally enslaved. He commented on the pass given by the Governor General of Cuba: "It contains on the face an untruth. The Governor General has not given a pass for *these* Negroes. And consequently these *bozales* stand on the deck of the *Amistad* without any *passo* whatever."[4]

Judge Judson then discussed source of this mystery:

Who sold these *bozales* to Don José Ruiz and took his twenty thousand dollars from him? I know not, but if he does, there is

his remedy. It is the sale of an article of goods to which he, the
seller, had no title.

And suppose this seller has absconded, or refuses to refund the
money, it may be a hard case for Mr. Ruiz, and yet *caveat emptor*
is the well known maxim, and he must set them down by the loss,
as many others are obliged to do. The purchaser must be vigilant
in the investigation of the property he buys. If there had been
vigilance in this case Ruiz and Montes might have saved all their
property, and the imminent hazard of life, and this court might
have been relieved from this heavy responsibility, which has been
pressing down on it for these four months.

Why did they not ascertain that these Negroes were *bozales?*
This has been the source of their complicated sufferings, the tale
of which will make the stoutest heart bleed! Why did they not
ascertain that the law of Spain had declared these objects of their
purchase not slaves?

The secret is told in a word. In Cuba it is the custom to buy
such Negroes, and ship them as *ladinos* or *creoles* and there respectable men have grown up under the influence of this custom;
this practice is against law.[5]

Judge Judson said the Spaniards could not come into an
American court, whether they knew their own law or not, and
expect that court to invade the rights of others in justification
of their breach of their own laws.

"Shall these *bozales* be given up under the treaty?" he asked.
"And if so, for what purpose? To have the question tried *there,*
whether they are slaves by the law of Spain? The Spanish law
declared that they are not slaves; it would be utterly useless,
then, to send them back to Cuba."

He digressed for a moment to discuss the question of Antonio,
the cabin boy slave of Captain Ferrer. Since Antonio was a
creole, and since he was the legal slave of Captain Ferrer,
Antonio would be returned to Cuba, to the proper heirs of
Captain Ferrer.

But the Africans, the real Africans, would be turned over to
the President of the United States to be shipped back to

Africa as free men, as the law of 1819 had decreed should be done in the case of Africans illegally enslaved.

The judge's review and decision took more than an hour. He concluded: "Cinqueze [Singbe] and Grabeau [Gilabaru] shall not sigh for Africa in vain. Bloody as may be their hands, they shall yet embrace their kindred. I shall put in form a decree of this Court, that these Africans, excepting Antonio, be delivered to the President of the United States to be transported to Africa, there to be delivered to the Agent appointed to receive and conduct them home."[6]

The battle for the Africans' freedom seemed to have been won.

14/Why They Called Martin Van Buren "Slave Dealer"

On February 10, 1840, just about a month after Judge Judson had handed down his unexpected verdict of freedom for the Africans, the Hartford *Courant* published a report culled from an anti-Van Buren newspaper, attacking the President for his stand on the *Amistad* case. The headline read:

MARTIN VAN BUREN TURNED SLAVE DEALER —

GROSS INTERFERENCE WITH OUR COURTS OF JUSTICE

The text was scarcely more temperate:

We are informed by a gentleman from New Haven that a short time previous to the trial of the Africans of the *Amistad*, before the U.S. District Court at New Haven, Judge Judson presiding, Martin Van Buren addressed a letter to the Judge recommending and urging him to order the Africans to be taken back to Havana in a government vessel, *to be sold there as slaves* — and that about the same time the U.S. schooner *Grampus* was ordered to New Haven for the purpose of receiving them. The schooner, we learned from several sources, arrived at New Haven about the time of the trial under *"sealed orders"* and, after learning the decision of the court again, "made off." The letter of the President, recommending that these poor unfortunate Africans be sent into *perpetual bondage,* is said to contain statements

167

disgraceful to the high station of its author, and which, were they published, would excite the indignation of every Republican freeman in the land. What will the friends of liberty say to this? Surely Martin Van Buren is playing the part of a *tyrant* with a high hand — else why this tampering with our courts of justice, this Executive usurpation, and this heartless violation of the inalienable rights of man? Of the truth of the above there is no doubt, and we leave the unprincipled author of such a proceeding in the hands of a just and high-minded People.[1]

The political compaign of 1840 was begun, and in spite of everything Martin Van Buren had done to keep the *Amistad* affair from becoming an issue in that campaign, he was to be plagued with it until long after the election.

The writer of the article had a grain or two of truth, but he used it in an attempt to assassinate the political Van Buren rather than to assess the case the *Amistad* captives had raised and the issues the case posed for American justice. Martin Van Buren was not a lover of slavery or a toady to the slaving interests; he was a master politician, and the issue of slavery was one he had long before chosen to try to live with rather than fight. Using his executive power, he had attempted to settle the question of the *Amistad* in a manner that would obviate international and national complications. He was resigned, early in the case, to accepting the slings and arrows of the abolitionists, but in this period the abolitionists had already earned themselves a name as over-eager zealots, if not outright fanatics. Of course, one man's fanatic was another man's hero: not all the abolitionists were also firm advocates of temperance and sworn enemies of rum; not all of them were fiery pastors or strong-minded vestrymen; but many of them were. The Arthur and Lewis Tappans and the Reverend Jocelyn, and the others who would station a hundred men and a ship in New Haven to spirit the captives away if the verdict went against them — these were the symbols of abolition.

The verdict in the *Amistad* case was handed down on January

13. One day before, Secretary of State Forsyth had written to District Attorney Holabird, telling him to carry out his orders, which were to put the Negroes on board the *Grampus,* just as soon as the verdict was received, if it was the verdict the Administration wanted. If the case went the other way—and the Administration had a very small fear that it might — the District Attorney was to appeal immediately.[2]

When the verdict came — Secretary Forsyth wrote again, worried, as a man worries when there is much at stake, that the first letter might have gone astray. He wrote a third time on January 17, ordering Holabird to appeal the branch of the decision that freed the Negroes and the branch of the decision that granted salvage on the ship and cargo. The part that concerned the slave Antonio was to be accepted.[3]

The Administration had patently been in touch with the Spanish minister again, concerned about the effect of the verdict on Spanish-American relations. These relationships grew more tense each year, partly as a result of the awareness and increased interests of the American people in the world south of them and the comparatively heavy volume of American sea trade. The United States needed good relationships with the Spanish government more than Spain needed them with the United States, and this need was very much in the mind of President Van Buren and his cabinet. Thus, knowing that the *Amistad* affair had blown up a storm and would blow up a worse one if it were kept in the public eye, the President felt impelled to appeal the court decision, and, after the decision, to reaffirm his demand for appeal.

The owners of the *Amistad* were inclined to sell off the schooner and its cargo for what it would bring, and District Attorney Holabird was ordered to facilitate this move, even if the money had to be put in escrow for the final decision of the courts.

But President Van Buren would never have undertaken the matter had he realized how tumultuous the effect of the Administration's conduct after January 13 would be. Indeed, so dreadful were the consequences of the *Amistad* affair to the fortunes of the Democrats and of Martin Van Buren that it became one of those issues to which he did not once refer in his *Autobiography,* which he began in Sorrento fourteen years later.

The tumult began on the day Judge Judson announced his verdict. The abolitionists in the crowd could scarcely believe that their old enemy would rule in their favor, but Judge Judson was a judge first of all and only second a citizen with the then common fault of race prejudice against Negroes; and this case involved principle and not the settlement of Negroes as his next door neighbors.

On hearing the judgment, the Reverend H.G. Ludlow hurried from the courtroom to the jail. Mr. Ludlow was a devout Protestant and an abolitionist, a member of the New Haven committee to assist the *Amistad* captives. Moving as rapidly as ministerial decorum allowed, he made his way around the green and to the jail, where he told the interpreter James Covey, who told the Africans the good news. All but one of them prostrated themselves at the feet of Mr. Ludlow. The one who did not move did not understand Mendi. When he was informed in another dialect, he too was down on his face, in gratitude for salvation.

The attitude elsewhere was quite the opposite. The Washington *Globe,* the official Administration newspaper, printed part of a letter from a Southern political leader who was not identified (students suspected it was F.W. Pickens of South Carolina): "This is the justice of an American Court, bowed down in disgraceful subserviency before the bigoted mandates of that blind fanaticism, which prompted the Judge upon the bench to declare in his decree, in reference to one of these Negroes, that, although he might be stained with crime, yet he should not sigh in vain for Africa; and all because his hands were reeking with the blood of murdered white men. It is a base outrage (I can use no milder language) upon all the sympathies of civilized life."[4]

The amazement of the South was even greater when it was realized that Judge Judson was a Van Buren appointee and the same man who had brought the criminal proceedings against Prudence Crandall for first accepting a colored student and then establishing a Negro boarding school.[5]

The appeal was filed and the parties sat down to wait again for the grinding of the wheels of justice.

The wheels of the American political machines were grinding all the while, too.

In March, so great was the excitement about the *Amistad* affair, and so many and serious were the rumors about the Administration's role, that John Quincy Adams arose in the House of Representatives and offered a resolution, asking to make available to the House, "if not incompatible with the public interest, copies of any demand made by the [Spanish] minister or any other diplomatic representative of Spain in this country, of the surrender to him of the Africans taken in or belonging to the vessel called the *Amistad*; and of all correspondence between this government and the said minister or diplomatic representative, and with any other foreign government or minister thereof, relating thereto; also, copies of all instructions from the Department of State to the district attorney of the United States in the judicial district of Connecticut, and all reports of the said district attorney to the said department relating to that subject."[6]

On March 23 the resolution was passed, and eight days later President Van Buren presented the House of Representatives with copies of the correspondence and papers in the Administration's files, except the current correspondence that dealt with the government's appeal of the court decision; that was withheld because to deliver it would be to give the lawyers for the Africans full knowledge of the case the government was trying to make.

The House ordered the printing of the correspondence and papers as House Document No. 185, 26th Congress, 1st Session, and made them available to Congressmen and the public. In a few days the entire printing was exhausted.

The New London *Gazette* heard some of the rumors about Judge Judson and the Administration and began to make inquiries. It had been charged earlier that Judge Judson had received a letter from President Van Buren trying to persuade him to turn his decision for the Spaniards. Judge Judson denied flatly that he had received any letter from the President on that or any other subject.

But why, asked a writer to the editor of the *Gazette*, was the ship *Grampus* dispatched so hastily to New Haven during the trial? The writer seemed to know. The *Grampus*, he said, arrived in New Haven in a condition entirely unfit for sea. He would be glad if someone would tell him "why she touched at New Haven just long enough for a boat to communicate with the shore; and why it was that the officers and others connected with her stated freely while here that they were destined for the coast of Africa, and were, as they believed, to take the *Amistad* Negroes?"

"Now, sir," the writer went on, "I conversed with one of the gentlemen connected with her, who told me that in coming from New Haven here she made three feet of water in the hold, in consequence of being hurried away from New York without being half fitted (being just out of dry dock). It is also well known to our citizens that she hauled herself alongside the wharf, recaulked with the utmost speed, and used every exertion to get ready for the sea in the earliest time possible."[7]

The writer saw improper connections between the decision of Judge Judson and the appearance of the *Grampus* — but he did not read them at all as the abolitionists had read them. He continued:

> Now, sir, it appears to me to be of little consequence to know whether instructions came from Washington or whether the case was decided before trial and its decision transmitted thither — if either supposition be true (and the facts have a strong squinting that way) the people should know it. The stride which the President has made towards universal power in other branches of the

government render it by no means improbable that he has at length
assumed the duties of the Judiciary, and that the case was decided at Washington long before the trial, and the *Grampus* held
in readiness to remove the Negroes the moment the court completes
the *forms* of the trial.

I cannot but hope, sir, that this view of the subject is a mistaken
one; for if it be true, our Federal Courts have become the mere
instruments of the President, and if this case was prejudged without the hearing either of the testimony or argument, what security
is left us for our property or liberties?

Until the movements of the *Grampus* are explained there will
remain in the minds of many, even of those who are friends of
the Administration, a painful suspicion of foul play.[8]

The answers to the questions about the movement of the
Grampus were contained in the papers released in House of
Representatives Document No. 185, which was reprinted, with
annotations, by the American Anti-Slavery Society and sold at its
bookstore on Nassau Street in New York City for 12½ cents a
copy. But what questions and fears the publication of the facts
allayed in the minds of "friends of the Administration" were
more than doubled by the fears and outcries of the Administration's enemies and the fiery abolitionists.

In the spring, as the case of the *Amistad* captives pended,
Circuit Court Judge Thompson refused to admit the captives
to bail — not even the four children — which action caused a
new outcry, furthered by a long editorial comment on the inside cover of the Anti-Slavery Society reprint that was published
a few weeks later, addressed grandly "To The People of the
United States":

The attention of the free people of this country is invited to the
contents of this public document, and they will not fail to notice
with astonishment the attempt of the executive to interfere with
the regular administration of justice. The Government of a free
people should protect defenseless strangers thrown, by the providence of God, after a successful struggle for liberty, upon their

shores, and not give them up to foreign claimants unless imperiously required to do it by treaty. But in this instance, it will appear that instead of interposing the national Aegis to shield the weak and oppressed, our government has lent all the aid and facilities at its command to have them placed in the hands of the Spaniards, with certain knowledge that many of them would be put to death. These Africans are detained in jail, under process of the United States Courts, in a free State, after it has been decided by the District Judge, on sufficient proof, that they are recently from Africa — were never the lawful slaves of Ruiz or Montes — that the libels of these Spanish claimants should be dismissed with costs — and when it is clear as noon-day that there is no law or treaty stipulation that requires the further detention of these Africans or their delivery to Spain or its subjects. And this, on the demand of the Spanish minister, who has been allowed to come into an American court and appeal, when the parties themselves — his countrymen — have made no appeal from the righteous decision of the District Court![9]

In his notes and comments at the foot of the pages, the Anti-Slavery Society editor was free with his criticisms of the Administration and quick to impugn President Van Buren's motivations.

At the beginning of the *Amistad* affair there was very little knowledge, by court or counsel, of the habits and slaving practices of the Spaniards in Cuba. It took the deposition testimony of Dr. Madden, the British official, to clarify the differences between *creoles, ladinos,* and *bozales.* So, when District Attorney Holabird had the ship's papers translated and copies sent to Washington, and the word *ladinos* was translated as "sound Negroes," there was reasonable ground to believe it was an honest error. Certainly the Spaniards and the Spanish authorities would not go out of the way to explain the corrupt practices of the Spanish administration of Cuba.

Yet the abolitionist editor of the document erupted in indignation when he came across this mistranslation. "This is a fraudulent translation," he said, and called attention to the deposition by Dr. Madden, which was made two weeks after the papers were sent to Washington. "And this is contained in a public document," thundered the editor, "transmitted to Congress by the President of the United States, and published by the authority of the House of Representatives!"[10]

The editor was very insulting to Attorney General Grundy (later Senator Grundy of Tennessee) in commenting on Grundy's opinion on the obligations of the United States under the treaty with Spain to return the ship and the captives: "What evidence this opinion furnishes of the fitness of the gentleman for the high office of Attorney General, members of the legal profession may determine. It is sufficient to say that it is contrary to the opinions of the most eminent jurists this country has produced, and it would seem that a lawyer who would venture on promulgating such doctrines was unfit to be even an attorney of the most inconsiderable district of the United States."[11]

Incontinent as were these remarks, the editors of the Anti-Slavery Society did uncover and point up one serious breach of the spirit, if not of the letter, of the American laws by the Administration. There in the pages of House of Representatives Document No. 185 was the sordid story of the calling up of the *Grampus* under secret orders on what might have become a most ignoble mission.

On January 6, just before the reconvening of the District Court in New Haven, Secretary of State Forsyth wrote to District Attorney Holabird, referring to a letter that was not included in the correspondence submitted to the House of Representatives. Obviously, in this Holabird letter of December 20, the district attorney had suggested the employment of an American ship, as requested by the Spanish minister, to be ready to take the Negroes to Cuba. The Secretary of State and the President accepted this idea eagerly, knowing what they were about, as was evident in the Secretary's letter of January 6: " . . . a vessel to be in readiness to receive the Negroes from the custody of the marshal as soon as their delivery shall have been ordered by the court . . . . "[12]

Five days later District Attorney Holabird was desperately writing back, for in preparing the order for the dispatch of the *Grampus* the words circuit court had been substituted for district court. "Should the pretended friends of the Negroes obtain a writ of habeas corpus, the marshal could not justify under the warrant," the worried district attorney wrote.

The error was corrected in haste, and Secretary Forsyth wrote to the district attorney on January 12: "With reference to the inquiry from the marshal, to which you allude, I have to state, by direction of the President, that if the decision of the court is such as is anticipated, the order of the President is to be carried into execution unless an appeal shall actually have been interposed. You are not to take it for granted that it will be interposed. . . . "[13]

The editor of the Anti-Slavery Society was completely aroused by the time he reached this evidence of official perfidy. "Mark this!" his footnote shouted. " 'You are not to take it for granted that it [an appeal] will be interposed.' That is if the counsel for the Africans do not enter an appeal *instanter*, the Africans are to be hurried on board the U.S. schooner *Grampus* and taken to Cuba — there to be made a terrific example to terrify the *bozale* Negroes not to make a similar strike for liberty!"

One more footnote was appended to the end of the document, chiding the Administration for its error in confusing circuit and district courts in the warrants to Marshal Wilcox and ending on a typical note of abolitionist determination: "The good providence of Almighty God has hitherto protected these unfortunate Africans. Prayer is daily ascending on their behalf. A strong and anxious sympathy is felt in the community, and it will not be the fault of those who have expended much time and money in their defense, or of the eminent counsel who have been and will be employed, if the Africans shall be given up to the tender mercies of the Spaniards."[14]

The purpose of the abolitionists was dual: they wished to save the Negroes' bodies from the lashes and garroters or hangmen of Havana; they wished to save their souls for Jesus Christ, and particularly to rescue those who had succumbed to the rival Islamic religion, which was so much the more anathema to the evangelists than simple paganism.

As winter settled in on New Haven, the interest in the captives did not die. The story of their case was dramatized, first at the Bowery Theater of New York, in a play called *The Black Schooner, or, The Pirate Slaver Amistad.* The play was so successful it ran for many days (in a time when plays changed very frequently) and brought in $1,650 in ticket sales. The scene of the play was the *Amistad,* with a cast that represented the captain, the mulatto slave, the two passengers Don José and Don Pedro, and all the slaves, plus the officers and crew of the brig *Washington.*[15]

For a time the play was performed at Niblo's Gardens, and then at the National Theater. Everywhere it was successful.

An artist named A. Hewins of Boston portrayed 26 of the characters of the drama on 135 square feet of canvas — a large painting by anyone's appraisal — and entitled it "The Massacre." It showed Singbe and the others killing Captain Ferrer. It was exhibited, with an admission charge, in New Haven and Hartford, and drew rave reviews from the press. The New Haven *Herald* described the painting in some detail. The New Haven *Palladium* said it "doubtless represents the bloody tragedy much as it was enacted." The New Haven *Register* counseled, "Go and see it." The New England *Review* in Hartford noted that it showed Singbe attacking Don Pedro: "He is held back by the interference of others and all the spirit of desperation and demoniacism is pictured in his expressive face."[16]

The *Amistad* captives were widely celebrated and became famous throughout the land through the efforts of the abolitionists, who used this case to strengthen their cause immeasurably. Through his interest, John Quincy Adams lent respectability to the matter, and Roger Sherman Baldwin, who also served during his lifetime as governor of Connecticut, made his reputation and

created a place for himself in New England history by his conduct as principal counsel for the defense in the early stages of
the affair.

As winter became spring, the one who was most hurt by
the entire episode was Martin Van Buren. The *Amistad* affair
added greatly to the heap of charges Van Buren's enemies
built up against him, charges that he had interfered in the legislative and judicial processes and had attempted to tyrannize the
people. Such charges were not uncommon in elections: they
had been made against John Quincy Adams when he was President, and they had been made against Andrew Jackson, Van
Buren's predecessor and mentor.

In the fall, Van Buren would go down to defeat at the hands
of William Henry Harrison (Tippecanoe and Tyler, too). What
part, could one say, did the *Amistad* affair play in the defeat?
It would be hard to attribute any specific number of votes or the
actions of states to this case, but one reason for Van Buren's
defeat was the growing belief that he had become too arrogant
in power; and the *Amistad* affair, and particularly the calling
up of the *Grampus,* was used widely and effectively against him
in this context.

Equally important — more important in the long run of American history — the election compaign of 1840 marked the first
campaign in which the slavery issue was formally made a part
of the political platform of any major American party. The southern Democrats insisted on, and obtained, a plank in the party
platform that pledged Democrats against the interference with
slavery in any manner by Congress. The national furor over the
Amistad affair was not the cause of this plank, any more than
the flood of petitions on slavery that had led to the Gag Rule,
but the case of the Negroes kept the issue of slavery uncomfort-
ably before the eyes of all Americans and the world, and in this
sense it contributed to the growing concern over the whole
question of man's right to be free.

15/In Captivity

As the months wore on, the *Amistad* captives began to acquire some knowledge of English. Their education was largely confined to the Bible and religious affairs, but it was still an education in the language, and a few of their teachers were interested in learning something about Africa and the Africans as well as in using them to fight an American institution and proselytizing for their salvation.

As snow covered the New Haven green and brought the square to its most beautiful, the abolitionists began to question the Africans. Had they seen snow? Yes, they said, they had seen snow, but not very much of it. Had they seen white men in their country? Yes, some said — referring to Don Pedro Blanco and other slavers. No, others said, there had never been a white man deep in Mendi country. Three African explorers, Park, Landers, and Winterbottom, had come near this land, but none had penetrated it; that is why in such works as Park's, with which Professor Gibbs had come to the jail on his first visit, there was only the sketchiest discussion of this land and nothing at all about the language.

The Africans instructed the whites in some of their customs, but the whites were more interested in imparting American civi-

179

lization to the Negroes and they spent from two to five hours each day in instruction.

Naturally the quickest to learn were the children, and it was not many weeks before they were chattering in quite an acceptable, though heavily accented, English. The adults took more time, and some, whose attention span was short, seemed never to learn more than a few words.

As in all else, Singbe took the lead and maintained order in the classrooms. But this problem was not a very serious one, as was noted in a description by one teacher: "Sometimes they complained because we did not come earlier, and refused consent to our departure when at noon or night it became necessary for us to leave. . . . Not infrequently in their desire to retain their teacher through the day, they attempt even to hold him, grasping his hands and clinging to his person, and individuals offer to give him their own dinner on condition of his remaining. Sometimes they may be found gathered in two or three groups, all reading and aiding each other. While the teacher is hearing one class, the interpreter is engaged in the same duty with another, and one of the most advanced among the captives gives instructions to another, and thus employed they sit for hours in the most patient, persevering effort to learn 'Merica'."[1]

The routine of life in jail was simple. In the morning they had breakfast and made their beds and cleaned the rooms in which they lived. When the teachers arrived, there were prayers, said while kneeling on the floor (if the room was large enough). The teacher would pray in English, James Covey would interpret in Mendi, and the Africans would respond in Mendi.

> O Great God,
>   O ga-wa-wa.
> Thou art Good,
>   bi-a-bi yan-ding-o.
> Thou hast made all things,
>   bi-a-bi ha-ni gbe-le ba-te-ni.

Then, after prayers, half an hour was spent, with Covey assisting the missionary-minded abolitionists, trying to persuade the Africans to Christian belief. On Sunday there were two such sessions, and once, when Covey was not available, Singbe conducted the services himself — but more as a matter of form than of religious fervor.

Spring wore into summer, and as the captives continued to be exercised on the New Haven green it was not too long before the general public began to lose interest in them — the novelty had disappeared.

The cost of maintaining the prisoners at subsistence level was paid by the federal government, which kept them imprisoned, but the cost of the extras, of their teaching and the propaganda in their behalf, and above all, of their defense, was paid by the volunteer committee headed by the Tappans. By summer, when it became very warm in New Haven and the jail was to be torn down, the marshal was persuaded to allow them to be held at Westville, two miles outside the city.

Of the forty-nine Africans who had left Cuba in the hour of their desperation, thirty-six were alive, the others having succumbed to the captain's sword, to gorging, and to disease. Most of the men spent their waking days in study or contemplation and by summer some of them were beginning to write faltering sentences in English.

A reporter from the Boston *Recorder* visited the Westville establishment and came away quite surprised to find that the Africans' teachers believed them to be the mental equal of white men.

"With one or two exceptions," he wrote, "they all have active minds and are quick, shrewd and intelligent. They possess deep and warm affections. Their love of Africa and home is very strong; in reply to a question put to two of the most intelligent of their number, the instant and deep-feeling answer was, 'Tell the American people that we very, *very* much want to go home.' Poor fellows! Who can doubt it?"

The hopes of the abolitionists were also reflected in this interview: "They are also uncommonly susceptible of religious impressions." The truths of the Bible they have already learned exert a greater or less influence on all of them. . . . They came here savages; but by the Divine blessing on the labors with them, they are now becoming civilized, and, it is hoped, Christian men."

But the problem of making them Christians and saving their souls, and getting them home to Africa and saving their bodies, was a vexatious one. The Tappans could not be expected to bear the entire expense for this service — they had far too many other anti-slavery irons in the fire.

The Christian reporter of the Boston *Recorder* called upon the Christian community to help solve this problem. He made an outright appeal for funds, explaining that the committee was in debt and that contributions should be sent to Amos Townsend, treasurer, in New Haven. The appeal was widely circulated by abolitionist newspapers.[2]

The presence of the African was not required in the Circuit Court case, since it was an appeal of judgment and the facts of the case had been established. They remained in Westville under the charge of Marshal Wilcox and jailer Pendelton.

In the summer the case on appeal was completed before Judge Thompson, who had heard the original question of the habeas corpus, and on September 17 he handed down his verdict: the appeal of the government was denied.

The lawyers saw the next step clearly. The government could have dropped the *Amistad* question, but all the political harm that could be done was done, and President Van Buren had given orders that the case was to be carried to the Supreme Court of the United States.

District Attorney Holabird lost no time in filing his formal appeal of the Circuit Court judgment. The Supreme Court would not meet until January, and so could not consider the *Amistad* case until after the election. Van Buren was hoping that the fight against the abolitionists would bring him at least the loyalty of the slaveholding South; or, to put it another way, he was nearly bound by the sense of the Democratic platform, if not its letter, to do exactly as he did.

The lawyers made ready for another expensive struggle. The *Amistad* and the goods aboard were sold at public auction that autumn; and the ship became a coasting schooner in Long Island Sound under another name, to disappear from the public eye.

Once the appeal of the federal government to the Supreme Court was announced, it was apparent to the Tappans and the other *Amistad* committee members that men of stature must continue the argument. Roger Sherman Baldwin, chief of counsel, was chosen to argue before the court, and John Quincy Adams was also asked to represent the Africans, for several reasons.

John Quincy Adams rose to full stature as a statesman only after he had left the Presidency of the United States. During his term of office as Chief Executive he was damned as the President who had defeated Andrew Jackson by making what was called a "corrupt deal" with Henry Clay to win Clay's voting support in the House of Representatives (where the election had to be decided because it was so close). In exchange for votes, John Quincy Adams had given Clay the coveted post of Secretary of State. Such deals were to become commonplaces of American political society in the years of the two-party system, but the Adams election preceded the two-party system, and what was acceptable later brought frowns of shock to the faces of many men who considered themselves to be right-thinking citizens. The Adams administration, then, lived always under a suspicion of corruption that was not justified in fact, and the voters turned him out of office by a large margin in 1828.

Following this defeat, and a period in which his name was scarcely respected even in his native New England, John Quincy Adams began a new career at the age of sixty-three with election to the House of Representatives in 1830. As a member of Congress he firmly championed what he believed to be right, such as freedom of speech and assembly; and firmly fought what he believed to be wrong, such as the theory of nullification of federal laws by states that disagreed with them, and the Gag Rule.

In 1840, when Adams was asked to carry the *Amistad* case before the Supreme Court, his views on slavery were "moderate," as the Southerners would say. He was not an abolitionist. What he proposed was the presentation of the issue of abolition to the people of the United States as a Constitutional amendment. He did not even particularly espouse the abolition of slavery in the District of Columbia at this time. So strong by 1840 were Southern feelings on the question of slavery that Adams's position was often misrepresented. He was called a "howling abolitionist" and "slave-lover," but this represented the hysteria of the South, and not the fact. The fact was that Adams was liked no better by the abolitionists than by the Southerners and was called "the Madman of Massachusetts" in abolitionist circles.

Some of the abolitionists were very leery of offering the task of counsel to John Quincy Adams because of his views. Some members of Adams' family were very leery of his accepting the offer because of the strange nature of the case. They thought it could bring him nothing but trouble.[3] But to Adams, here was a clear-cut matter of principle, which he had stated in his letters to the editors of newspapers early in the development of the legal case. He was determined to accept the responsibility when it was offered to him at the end of October, 1840.

In November, Adams and Baldwin conferred in New Haven about the case. Baldwin would write the brief and would submit an argument of his own. Adams would sum up for the Africans.

On this visit to New Haven, Adams visited the Africans at Westville. Then he went on to Washington to prepare the argument of the case.

Effort was made to stop the case, now that the election was over. Van Buren had been defeated and he seemed to have nothing to lose. He said the case must come to a logical conclusion — the Spanish minister insisted.

John Quincy Adams devoted much of his time to the *Amistad* problem and all its straggling detail. He saw Henry Gilpin, new Attorney General in the Van Buren cabinet who had replaced Senator Grundy. He went to see Secretary of State Forsyth and found him very angry about the misrepresentation made by the abolitionists in their reprinting of House Document No. 185. An investigation had been conducted into the misuse of the word *ladino*, and it had all devolved onto a proofreader; but abolitionists continued to accuse the Administration, and particularly the Secretary of State, of bad faith and dishonesty in the translations.

Consequently, any chance there might have been (and it must have been a slim one) of getting the case dismissed by consent was made impossible by the excesses of Lewis Tappan and his friends.

Adams talked to many people as he prepared his argument. He received a visit from the British minister, Henry Stephen Fox, who asked his help in drafting a letter to the President about the *Amistad* case to show Britain's abiding interest in the right of the Negroes to be free.

Another day, Adams had an unexpected caller: "Miss Margaret Monroe Stuart came in — a maiden lady, who in the compass of half an hour uttered in one continuous stream more good words than I could record in three months. Her sister is the wife of Captain Gedney, who is here very sick, and, she fears, not very sound in mind. She came to entreat me that in arguing the *Amistad* case before the Supreme Court I would not bear hard upon Captain Gedney, for she fears it might kill him, and she is sure it would kill her sister. I assured her that I would have all due consideration for the condition of Captain Gedney."[4]

Early in his consideration of the legal factors in this case, John Quincy Adams realized that the issue would depend greatly, from the Supreme Court's point of view, on the body of law and legal decisions in similar cases. One day, while perusing materials in the files of the Supreme Court, he encountered Francis Scott Key, composer of "The Star-Spangled Banner," who was serving as United States District Attorney for the District of Columbia:

> He said he was afraid there was not any chance for the poor creatures; that the case of the *Antelope* was precisely in point against them. He had argued that case for the freedom of the Negroes but it had been overruled. Yet it would never do to send them back to Cuba. The best thing that could be done was to make up a purse, and pay for them, and then send them back to Africa.
>
> I said we hoped to prove that the case of the *Antelope* would not be conclusive in its bearings upon our clients; but he continued very positive that it would. I went, therefore, into the Supreme Court library room and took out the volume of Wheaton's Reports containing the case of the *Antelope*. I read as much of it as I could, and longed to comment upon it as I could; but I have neither time nor head for it — nothing but heart.[5]

When the *Antelope* had reached American waters in 1819, captured and brought into Savannah harbor by a United States cruiser, it had two hundred Negroes aboard. About twenty-five had been captured from an American slave ship; the rest had been taken from Spanish and Portuguese slavers. Since slavery was then legal in Portugal and Spain, the governments of those two nations demanded the return of the slaves captured from their ships, saying that the capture constituted an act of piracy. The United States District Court adjudged the plaintiffs right in their contention, and the slaves of the Portuguese and Spanish ships were ordered returned. The case was appealed to the United States Circuit Court and the judgment was affirmed.

Then a serious difficulty developed. In the course of the travels of the *Antelope* the slaves had become intermixed and no one could say for certain which slaves came from the Spanish, which from the Portuguese, and which from the American slave ships. Circuit Court Judge Johnson of South Carolina decided that the slaves must draw lots and accept the burdens fate

placed upon them. Lots were drawn and the slaves were allo-
cated. The lottery was disallowed, however, when the United
States Supreme Court threw it out as improper. The Spanish
and Portuguese were to have their slaves, under the law, but
they would have to identify them to get them.[6]

If John Quincy Adams needed motivation — and he did
not — he would have had plenty of it in the letter written to him
by Ka-le, one of the African children. Ka-le was eleven years
old and had learned to read and write English far better than
any of the other *Amistad* captives. On the eve of the Supreme
Court hearings this lad understood only too well what the efforts
of John Quincy Adams would mean, and he bent himself over
paper and pen long and hard to produce a letter to his white
friend, a letter dated at New Haven on January 4, 1840.

> Dear Friend Mr. Adams:
> I want to write a letter to you because you love Mendi people,
> and you talk to the grand court. We want to tell you one thing.
> José Ruiz say we born in Havana, he tell lie. We stay in Havana
> 10 days and 10 nights, we stay no more. We all born in Mendi —
> we no understand the Spanish language. Mendi people been in
> America 17 moons. We talk American language a little, not
> very good; we write every day; we write plenty letters; we read
> most all time; we read all Matthew, and Mark, and Luke, and
> John, and plenty of little books. We love books very much.
> We want you to ask the court what we have done wrong.
> What for Americans keep us in prison. Some people say Mendi
> people crazy; Mendi people dolt, because we no talk America
> language. Merica people no talk Mendi language; Merica people
> dolt?
> They tell bad things about Mendi people, and we no under-
> stand. Some men say Mendi people very happy because they laugh
> and have plenty to eat. Mr. Pendleton come, and Mendi people
> all look sorry because they think about Mendi land and friends
> we no see now. Mr. Pendleton say Mendi people angry; white men
> afraid of Mendi people. The Mendi people no look sorry again —
> that why we laugh. But Mendi people feel sorry; O, we can't tell
> how sorry. Some people say Mendi people no got souls. When we
> feel bad, we got no souls: We want to be free very much.

Dear friend Mr. Adams, you have children, you have friends, you love them, you feel very sorry if Mendi people come and carry them all to Africa. We feel bad for our friends, and our friends all feel bad for us. Americans no take us in ship. We on shore and Americans tell us slave ship catch us. They say we make you free. If they make us free they tell true, if they no make us free they tell lie. If American people give us free we glad, if they no give us free we sorry — we sorry for Mendi people little, we sorry for American people great deal, because God punish liars. We want you to tell court that Mendi people no want to go back to Havana, we no want to be killed. Dear Friend, we want you to know how we feel. Mendi people *think, think, think.* Nobody know what he think; the teacher he know, we tell him some. Mendi people have got souls. We think we *know* God punish us if we tell lie. We never tell lie, we speak truth. What for Mendi people afraid? Because they got souls. Cook says he kill, he eat Mendi people — we afraid — we kill cook; then captain kill one man with knife, and cut Mendi people plenty. We never kill captain, he no kill us. If court ask who brought Mendi people to America? We bring ourselves. Ceci hold the rudder. All we want is make us free.

Your friend,
Ka-Le[7]

The abolitionists, who supervised the mailing of the letter, swore that the composition was entirely the boy's and that they had neither put him up to it nor told him how to phrase it. It could have been an effective document for propaganda, but it was not used by the abolitionists until after the case had been decided.

The briefs of both sides were in the hands of the Supreme Court justices, and it was agreed by Roger Baldwin and John Quincy Adams that they would first present a motion to dismiss the case on the grounds that the United States courts had no jurisdiction, no legal interest in the result of the case. Chief Justice Roger Brooke Taney had set January 16, 1841, as the date for argument of this motion, but Justice Joseph Story was absent on that day and it was put over for a few days until all the Supreme Court could be in attendance. The Chief Justice was very conscious of the intense national interest in this case and the effect it might have on American law regarding slavery.

John Quincy Adams was pleased to have the case delayed
because Congress was in session and he was also attending metic-
ulously, as always, to his Congressional duties, studying the
affairs of his committees and attending the sessions of the House.

One postponement followed another and it was not until
February 20 that the motion to dismiss the appeal was brought
before the Court, which had decided to hear both that motion
and the merits of the appeal as argued by Attorney General
Gilpin.

The attorney general opened with the statement that the
papers of the *Amistad* and those of all the Spaniards aboard
the *Amistad* were in proper order. The ship's bills of lading told
the story of the cargo. The unfortunate Captain Ferrer had pass-
ports for himself and his two Negro slaves, the cook and the
messboy. The two free members of the crew, unknown to the
court, were also properly registered. Don José Ruiz had his
passport and a license to transport his slaves; Don Pedro Montes
had the same.

The Negroes were held as slaves in a country where slavery
was legal. How they had strayed into United States territory
was known. If the Negroes were slaves, then they were property,
and as property the government of Spain had the right to demand restoration to the owners and to Spanish soil to be tried
for the crimes they had committed against Spanish law.

The case, said Attorney General Gilpin, was clear-cut and
pertinent to the law as established in the case of the *Antelope*.

There, in neat logic, was the essence of the Government case.
Regardless of what mistreatment there had been of the Spanish
law, under the treaty with Spain the United States was bound
to abide by the Spanish law and accept it.

Attorney General Gilpin spent all of the Saturday session discussing the merits of the case, and spoke again on Monday,
taking five hours to present his argument.

Roger Baldwin was to open for the defense because John
Quincy Adams felt he was not yet competent. "I was not half
prepared," he wrote in his diary, "and went to the court with

a heavy heart, full of undigested thought, sure of the justice of my cause, and deeply desponding of my ability to sustain it."[8]

And after hearing Attorney General Gilpin's argument on Monday, he wrote: "I walked to the Capitol with a thoroughly bewildered mind" [the Supreme Court was then in the Capitol building], "so bewildered as to leave me nothing but fervent prayer that presence of mind may not utterly fail me at the trial I am about to go through."[9]

Adams was a conscientious man, and he had reminded the abolitionists when they came to Quincy to see him that he had not argued a case before the high court in thirty years. He was certain that this case was the most important slavery case he had ever encountered. He was also certain that the Negroes of the *Amistad* must be freed in the interest of the good name of the United States, and he was deeply afraid that he was inadequate to the task and would fail to free them.

Baldwin opened for the *Amistad* captives on Monday, after saluting the court and noting its freedom from prejudice, "elevated far above the influence of Executive power and popular prejudice," as it was.[10]

During the last days before the trial, the pro-Administration newspaper, the *Globe,* had conducted a campaign obviously intended to influence all Washington and the Supreme Court itself. The *Globe* attacked Judge Judson for his original decision in the *Amistad* case and wrote harsh words about the captives. Further, President Van Buren had sent a letter to the Senate encompassing demands of the Spanish minister under the treaty of 1795 and containing articles from the Spanish press that called the *Amistad* captives murderers and pirates. Because these were put into an executive communication, they became part of the Congressional Record and were widely circulated in the press. All this, again, was patently an attempt to influence the decision of the Supreme Court.

Baldwin brought this information into his speech, denouncing it and adding that of course it would not influence the justices and would not tell on the scales of the justice about to be meted out by the highest court in the United States.

One vital issue, said Baldwin, and a new issue to Americans, was whether the United States government, which was founded on a concept of liberty, could become an instrument for the enslavement of people who were free at the moment that they stepped onto United States territory.

He briefly repeated the facts of the case, from the time the schooner sailed from Havana, in order to show how the *Amistad* captives had rebelled and seized control of the ship and were in control of it when it anchored off Culloden Point. He emphasized that most of the captives had been on shore in New York, where slavery was prohibited by law. He summed up the entire case in one paragraph:

> To these several libels, claims and suggestions, the Africans, who when seized were in the condition of freemen, capable of having and enforcing rights of their own, severally answered: that they were born free — and were kidnaped in their native country, and forcibly and unlawfully transported to Cuba; — that they were wrongfully and fraudulently put on board of the schooner *Amistad* by Ruiz and Montes, under color of permits *fraudulently* obtained and used; that after achieving their own deliverance, they sought an asylum in the State of New York, by the laws of which they were free; and that while there, they were illegally seized by Lieutenant Gedney, and brought into the District of Connecticut.

The point about Gedney's illegal actions bore repetition because it had not been made so solidly before.

Baldwin contended that the United States government was being called upon by the Spanish government to aid the Spanish in the recovery of fugitive slaves and that the American executive branch had no such right or responsibility. When the *Amistad* captives came to United States waters they were free, and they did not touch shore at a place where they could be enslaved; they were at a place where all persons except fugitives from sister states were declared to be free.

He also pointed to the ninth article of the treaty with Spain, which said that property should be returned to the owner of a vessel in distress *as soon as due and sufficient proof shall have been made concerning the property thereof.* The Africans had not been slaves when they were captured. They had been illegally enslaved by their captors in the first place, and illegally sold, and later illegally purchased in Havana.

Baldwin also maintained that the Spaniards Ruiz and Montes had made no effort in Cuba to recover their property:

> The evidence tends strongly to prove that Ruiz at least was concerned in the importation of these Africans, and that the re-shipment of them under color of passports obtained for *ladinos,* as the property of Ruiz and Montes, in connection with the false representation on the papers of the schooner, that they were *"passengers for the government,"* was an artifice resorted to by these slave traders for the double purpose of evading the scrutiny of British cruisers, and legalizing the transfer of their victims to the place of their ultimate destination. It is a remarkable circumstance, that though more than a year has elapsed since the decree of the District Court, denying the title of Ruiz and Montes, and pronouncing the Africans free, not a particle of evidence has since been produced in support of their claims. And yet — strange as it may seem – during all this time, not only the sympathies of the Spanish minister, but the powerful aid of our own Government have been enlisted in their behalf! [11]

When Baldwin finished his argument, late in the day on Tuesday, it was time for adjournment. All in the courtroom that day left with the feeling that Baldwin had been impressive — "sound and eloquent," as John Quincy Adams called him — but exceedingly mild. He had summed up the case admirably from the standpoint of law, and if the precedents of law were all that were to be concerned, the Baldwin argument should have carried the day.

Yet on the way back to his study that night, Adams felt that the Baldwin argument was somehow incomplete; that it did not face up to the actual conditions of the day in Washington and in the nation. If the *Amistad* case had not concerned issues that were growing in importance and heat in the United States, it would never have caused the stir it did. The slave-owners of the South were up in arms about the decision: they said it directly threatened the future of slavery in those parts of the United States where it had been legal for years, and some even conjured up visions of slaves escaping North to freedom in droves. The abolitionists were equally aroused: they said the Africans must be freed and that the United States government must not interfere in slave cases in behalf of slaveholders. Even the average non-slaveholding Americans who were not sufficiently aroused by the matters of slavery to become aboli-tionists were expressing concern over the *Amistad* case. Their reason was more simple, more direct, more dramatic. The *Amistad* captives had freed themselves from slavery once, vio-lent as that wrench may have been.

In the aimless wanderings of the *Amistad* Africans for two months upon the sea, had they fallen in with a British cruiser they would have been taken into a port straightaway, removed from the slave ship, and set free as persons illegally enslaved. Instead of finding a British captain who would have been five guineas richer for each head, the captives had run afoul of an ambitious American officer whose economic advancement would be furthered by their re-enslavement. Lieutenant Commander Gedney had every intention of pursuing his claim for salvage until, during the trial, he saw how unfavorable public opinion was growing against him. He asked his attorneys to disavow, publicly, the claim for salvage on the human beings.

The *Amistad* affair had assumed proportions far greater than the facts would suggest, and John Qiuncy Adams, from his long experience and his sense of history, understood the im-portance of the case. To be correct and legal was all very well, but here one must also deal with the world as it was in February, 1841, the real world that lay outside the Supreme Court portals, the world that would be deeply affected by the precedents set in that courtroom.

It was Wednesday, February 24, when balding John Quincy
Adams rose before the court, his wispy white hair and sideburns
flaring out around his clean-shaved face like a vertical halo;
and the deep lines that slanted outward from the base of his
nose and those that turned down the corners of his mouth were
sharper-edged than usual.

"I had been deeply distressed and agitated till the moment
when I rose; and then my spirit did not sink within me," he
wrote in his *Memoirs*.[12]

John Quincy Adams did not speak as a lawyer, as his pre-
decessors had done, but as a political leader, opening the case
far beyond the doors of the lawbooks, bringing the law and the
case into the context of the daily world.

He began by discussing justice, taking his hearers back to the
institutes of the Roman Emperor Justinian, from whom the word
was derived. He charged that the Van Buren administration
sought injustice: "The charge I make against the present Executive administration is that in all their proceedings relating to
these unfortunate men, instead of that *Justice*, which they were
bound not less than this honorable court to observe, they have
substituted Sympathy! — sympathy with one of the parties in
this conflict of justices, and *Antipathy* to the others. Sympathy
with the white, antipathy to the black — and in proof of this
charge I adduce the admission and avowal of the Secretary of
State himself. . . . "

He quoted a letter from Secretary Forsyth to Caballero Argaiz
that was sympathetic to Señor Ruiz and Señor Montes, and
then said: "All the proceedings in the matter, on the part both
of the Executive and Judicial branches of the government, have
had their foundation in the assumption that these persons alone
were the parties aggrieved; and that their claims to the surrender
of the property was founded in fact and in justice."

The sympathy with the Spanish, whom Adams referred to
as "slave-traders," had been apparent from the beginning and
had continued in the actions of the federal government. "By
what right," Adams asked, "all this sympathy, from Lieutenant

Gedney to the Secretary of State, and from the Secretary of State, as it were, to the nation, was extended to the two Spaniards from Cuba exclusively, and utterly denied to the fifty-two victims of *their* lawless violence?"

Here Adams came to the most important issue of national concern: "One of the judges, who presided in some of the preceding trials, is said to have called this an anomalous case. It is indeed anomalous, and I know of no law, but which I am not at liberty to argue before this Court, no law, statute or constitution, no code, no treaty, applicable to the proceedings of the Executive or the Judiciary, except that law —"

Adams paused dramatically and pointed his finger at a copy of the Declaration of Independence that hung against one of the pillars of the courtroom.

"— that law, two copies of which are ever before the eyes of Your Honors. I know of no other law that reaches the case of my clients, but the law of Nature and Nature's God on which our fathers placed our own national existence. The circumstances are so peculiar, that no code or treaty has provided for such a case. That law, in its application to my clients, I trust will be the law on which the case will be decided by this Court."[13]

It was wrong of Lieutenant Commander Gedney to seize the *Amistad* in the first place, Adams said. It was wrong that they were imprisoned, and most of all it was wrong that the district attorney, having written the Secretary of State, should attempt to persuade him to take action to prevent the case from being tried.

Doggedly, the former President cited the instances in which the government officials showed their hope that the Africans would be sent back to Havana as slaves. He named Secretary Forsyth and showed some of his correspondence on the subject, accusing the Secretary of State of having abused the truth. He commented strongly on the dubious truthfulness of the letter of the first Spanish minister, Don Añgel Calderon, on the affairs of the Africans.

But more significant than the question of the Africans, said

John Quincy Adams, was the question of the interference of the
Administration in the dispensation of justice in the United States:

> May it please Your Honors — if the President of the United
> States had arbitrary and unqualified power, he could not satisfy
> these demands [of the Spaniards]. He must keep them [the
> *Amistad* prisoners] as a jailer; he must then send them beyond seas
> to be tried for their lives. I will not recur to the Declaration of
> Independence — Your Honors have it implanted in your hearts —
> but one of the grievous charges brought against George III was
> that he had made laws for sending men beyond seas for trial.
> That was one of the most odious of those acts of tyranny which
> occasioned the American revolution. The whole of the reasoning
> is not applicable to this case, but I submit to Your Honors
> that, if the President had the power to do it in the case of Africans,
> and send them beyond seas for trial, he could do it by the same
> authority in the case of American citizens. By a simple order to
> the marshal of the district, he could just as well seize forty citizens
> of the United States, on the demand of a foreign minister, and
> send them beyond seas for trial before a foreign court.... [14]

Adams did not confine himself in this appeal to the innate
sense of justice of the Supreme Court; he went into the legal
aspects of the case, citing paragraph after paragraph of the
Spanish-American treaty and the body of United States law
applicable to this case.

Yet the most telling parts of his address were those that added
facts or interpretations of facts or new lights to this case. He
noted that when the slaves left Havana there were fifty-four of
them and that from their sufferings sixteen of them had died
before November, 1839, when they were in American hands
and the ill-effects of their voyage had worn off. After that time,
no more had died.

He spoke of the letter and spirit of the treaty, noting that
it was impossible to believe that when the treaty was drawn
the Americans writing it had any thought of slaves being listed
as *merchandise* under the treaty. He spoke with conviction and
authority — for he had been Secretary of State when the Spanish-
American treaty was renewed in 1819: "With regard to Article

9, I will speak of my own knowledge, for it happened that on
the renewal of the treaty in 1819, the whole of the negotiations
with the then minister of Spain passed through my hands, and
I am certain that neither of us ever entertained an idea that
this word *merchandise* was to apply to human beings."[15]

He said there was not a single article of the treaty that had
application in this case — and the court listened because he
knew the treaty and the context of its negotiations.

Adams went on to consider another charge advanced by the
Spanish government, the charge that unless the *Amistad* captives
were punished for murder the internal tranquility of Cuba would
be disturbed. He dismissed that quickly, showing it for what it
was, a veiled charge that failure to punish these slaves would
cause uprisings among the slaves of the United States in the
South.

It was apparent to him, he told the court, that verbal or
other communications had passed between the various parties
representing the federal government and Spain. (Indeed, it
is apparent that not all this information and instructions are in
House Document No. 185 because the House was careful to ask
only for the material it considered in the public interest.)

Many aspects of the case were suddenly illuminated in the
Adams's speech. Throughout the correspondence between government representatives, the Spanish minister had used the term
gubernativamente, which was not easily translated in English
because of its peculiar Spanish meaning. It meant, in effect,
the absolute authority of the central government to act by fiat, to
seize prisoners without hearing, without trial, and to ship them
overseas or anywhere, for any reason. Such, said John Quincy
Adams, was what the Spanish minister had called upon the
United States President to do.

He reviewed the case of the *Antelope*, arguing that it did
not apply to the *Amistad* captives. He devoted much time
to the details because he knew that it was to this case that the
court would most likely refer. One of his basic arguments was
that in the *Antelope* case the court was divided almost evenly,
with the weight of one justice's opinion deciding the case. Chief

Justice Marshall had said that "the Court is divided on it, and consequently no principle is settled"[16] — even though, after seven years of litigation and the decision that the Africans could not be enslaved by lot, thirty-nine were enslaved and delivered to the Spanish vice-consul because they had been so unlucky as to draw the wrong lots!

John Quincy Adams spoke all day: "With grateful heart for aid from above, though in humiliation for the weakness incident to the limits of my powers, I spoke four hours and a half, with sufficient method and order to witness little flagging of attention by the Judges or the auditory."[17]

Having attacked the Administration, having shown how it was unduly responsive to outrageous demand by the Spanish minister, his address was brought to a close by the adjournment of the court.

Next morning he returned, but there was a stir in the courtroom. The crowd assembled. The justices filed into the room, and Chief Justice Taney appeared sad and bemused. Then, when all were in the room, it was apparent that Mr. Justice Barbour of Virginia was not present.

The crier opened the court in his usual manner. Then Chief Justice Taney addressed the bar: "Gentlemen, a painful event has occurred. Judge Barbour died suddenly last night — and the court is therefore adjourned until Monday."[18]

The trial resumed on March 1. After the lawyers paid homage to Justice Barbour, John Quincy Adams continued his argument.

He introduced a statement made by District Attorney Holabird, recalling a conversation with Spanish Vice-Consul Vega of Boston, in which the Spanish official had said the law against bringing slaves to Cuba was basically inoperative and that everyone in Cuba knew that slaves were constantly being imported from Africa. Adams's point was that the authorities of Spain were constantly conniving at the illegal slave traffic and that this was all the more reason the court must not accept any claims by the Spanish government.

Having exhausted his arguments, having noticed that on this

second day his voice was not standing the strain as it had on the first and that there was rustling in the courtroom that betokened a certain impatience, John Quincy Adams summed up:

> I said, when I began this plea, that my final reliance for success in this case on this court as a court of *justice;* and in the confidence of this fact inspired that, in the administration of justice, in a case of no less important than the liberty and life of a large number of persons, this Court would not decide but on a due consideration of all the rights, both natural and social, of *every one* of these individuals. I have endeavored to show that they are entitled to their liberty from this Court. I have avoided, purposely avoided, and this Court will do justice to the motive for which I have avoided, a recurrence to those first principles of liberty which might well have been invoked in the argument of this cause. . . . I have shown that Ruiz and Montes, the only parties in interest here, for whose sole benefit this suit is carried on by the government, were acting at the time in a way that is forbidden by the laws of Great Britain, of Spain, and of the United States, and that the mere signature of the Governor General of Cuba ought not to prevail over the ample evidence in the case that these Negroes were free and had a right to assert their liberty. I have shown that the papers in question are absolutely null and insufficient as passports for persons, and still more invalid to convey or prove a title to property.
>
> The review of the case of the *Antelope* and my argument in behalf of the captives of the *Amistad* is closed.[19]

John Quincy Adams, old and tired, stood before the Court then and said his farewells. He recalled that he had had his name first inscribed in 1804 on the rolls of those permitted to practice before the Supreme Court, that he had last appeared there in 1809 before going abroad to serve his country, that he now stood for what must be the last time before the court, and wondered at how it had changed. He cited the names of justices of the past — Marshall, Cushing, Chase, among them — and lamented that all were dead while he alone of his generation

remained. He gave the court his final blessing, and then returned to his seat.

The counsel for Lieutenant Commander Gedney were ready
and eager to follow Adams, but Chief Justice Taney declined
to hear any discussion of the claim for salvage until the court
had decided on the motion to dismiss the case for lack of
jurisdiction — a motion that Baldwin and Adams had entered
at the beginning.

Attorney General Gilpin then closed the case, summing up
the appeal and taking much notice of Roger Sherman Baldwin's
legal arguments and very little notice of John Quincy Adams's
social, moral, and political ones.

The next week, on Friday at noon, as was the custom of the
court, the decision was announced. Adams, in Washington,
rushed to write to his associate counsel in New Haven:

> The decision of the Supreme Court in the case of the *Amistad*
> has this moment been delivered by Judge Story. The captives are
> free. Yours in great haste and great joy,
>
> J.Q. Adams[20]

Later, when the official records of the *Amistad* case were
published, the court noted that the arguments of Attorney General Gilpin and Roger Sherman Baldwin were given great weight
in the consideration of the *Amistad* affair, but that in the argument of John Quincy Adams, "many of the points presented
by Mr. Adams, in the discussion of the case, were not considered
by the court essential to its decision; and were not taken notice
of in the opinion of the court." Adams had not expected the arguments to carry great weight as legal argument. He had not even
submitted a copy of his argument or a brief or synopsis. He had
left the legal principles to Baldwin, and he had undertaken to
establish two points: first, the moral responsibility of the United
States Supreme Court to preserve and uphold the principles
of freedom in America; and second, the inapplicability of the
Antelope case to the affair under consideration. Obviously, he
had succeeded in both these endeavors, although this success

did not show itself in citations in the opinions of the members
of the court.

The news of freedom was two days in reaching New Haven.
The news reached Marshal Wilcox via the New York City newspapers and a steamboat. The old jail had been torn down and
the *Amistad* captives were being held yet in Westville, so Marshal Wilcox drove out to Westville to inform the captives of
the results of the trial.

"The big court say you all free. No slaves," he reported.
"Here it is in this paper. Read it."

Singbe spoke for all of them: "Me glad. Me thank the American men." He told Ka-le to read the article aloud.

Then he said thoughtfully, "Paper lie sometimes."

But within a matter of hours the abolitionists came in force,
first Mr. Ludlow and Mr. Townsend, and then others, and all
of them repeated the good news. The day was given over to
praying and to celebration of the deliverance.[21]

The decision of the court was to affirm the decisions of the
District and Circuit Courts regarding the *Amistad,* but not those
regarding the *Amistad* captives. They were declared free, not
at the disposal of the President of the United States to return to
Africa, but free immediately in the United States. They were
to be discharged from the custody of the United States Marshal
at once.

Adams wrote this good news to Lewis Tappan at the same
hour that he wrote to Roger Baldwin, and it was not long before
Tappan was aboard the next steamboat for the Connecticut city.

On receipt of Adams' letter, Baldwin immediately faced up
to the consequences of the Supreme Court ruling. What was
to be done with the *Amistad* captives now that they were free?
he asked in a letter written on March 12.

Adams replied that the federal government had a distinct
responsibility to look after them, "having by its military, executive, and judicial authorities deprived them of the means of
accomplishing that purpose." He said he thought a memorial
should be addressed to the President of the United States

asking that they be sent home at the expense of the government.

In Washington, Adams had encountered Judge Thompson and had applied for an order to the marshal of the District of Connecticut to discharge the prisoners. Judge Thompson had promised to deliver it on his return to the North.

Soon the important members of the *Amistad* committee were assembled in New Haven, and the work of restoring the captives to freedom began. New appeals were made for subscriptions to the captives fund. Freed, the Africans could be taken about the countryside for exhibition, to help raise money for themselves and for various abolitionist causes.

The case, at least the legal case, was now over and won.

16/The New Freedom

Where were the Africans to go, once they had been freed by the American government?

They could not simply go home; the money must be raised to send them. Or the government could undertake the expenses.

Members of the abolitionist community in Farmington, Connecticut, agreed to take the captives there, establish a place for them to live, teach them rudimentary skills, and improve their command of the English language and the Bible before they returned to Africa. They would be housed on the grounds of a man named A.F. Williams. He said he would build a dormitory for them, they would be given the use of rooms over the store belonging to one Edward Deming as classrooms.

Lewis Tappan was particularly insistent that the Africans be kept in the United States for a time because he wanted them to return to Africa as Christians and spread the evangelical faith. He also wanted the little girls freed to join the others. They were then, and had been, living with Pendletons as wards and servants.

For a few weeks the abolitionists were very busy trying to win the freedom of the little girls. Eventually, this became a problem so serious that the abolitionists took it to court. The

girls said they wanted to stay with the Pendletons. The abolitionists declared that the Pendletons were making slaves of them
and that the *Amistad* captives must have the opportunity to discuss with the children their real wishes. In New Haven County
Court the two sides argued, Roger Baldwin again representing
the Africans, and the argument revealed the extent to which
the jailer had prospered personally from the coming of the
Africans. He had pocketed much of the money charged for
admission to see the captives. He had participated in a scheme
by which wax figures of the captives were made and sent to
most of the large cities of the East for public (and paying)
exhibition. It was ascertained that the Pendletons had kept the
little girls afraid that if they went away with the others they
would be sold into slavery. All this came out in court, and
custody of the children was awarded to Amos Townsend, a New
Haven banker and member of the *Amistad* committee. They were
taken to a carriage, against their will, and driven immediately
to the train that would take them to Farmington.[1]

The decision was not popular in New Haven, especially as
the public saw how little the girls wished to accompany the
abolitionists. But there was nothing the people could do except
hiss and boo the abolitionists as they went — and this they did
with considerable fervor.

The Africans went to Farmington on the train, all together,
and when they arrived, they had new Christian names (except
for Singbe, who kept the name Joseph).

They were met by Lewis Johnson, George Lewis, Henry
Coweles, and Alexander Posey.

They were taken to the First Church of Farmington and
there were brought to front pews in an evening service already
begun. Only after the service were they allowed to go to the
barracks built for them on the Williams' land, for there was a
reason for their appearance at the church: the abolitionist-evan-
gelists wished to arouse the zeal of the white congregations of

the region for the establishment of a chain of missions in West Africa.[2]

Shortly after the *Amistad* captives were moved to Farmington, Antonio the slave escaped the custody of Colonel Pendleton and disappeared rather than return to the slavery he once said he preferred. The authorities searched for him, at the behest of Spanish diplomats in the United States, but except for the suspicion that he had been spirited away by the abolitionists, they had little on which to act. He was not found.

In Farmington, the Africans were, in a sense, in tighter confinement than they had been under the authorities in New Haven. The jailers in New Haven had no objection to snuff and rum, but the God-fearing abolitionists had much objection. It soon became apparent to the Africans that they were being kept for reasons other than their own comfort or safety, and they grew fretful. Singbe and others were taken to various cities — New York, Boston, Albany, — to be displayed and assist the fundraisers in their work. They did not like being put on display, and Singbe sometimes said as much, which did not make him popular with Lewis Tappan and abolitionist leaders.

Tragedy came to the Africans again in Farmington. Foone, one of the favorites of the whites, went swimming in the Center Basin one day. It was a pleasant place, a swimming hole where the Africans could cool off on the hot days of a Connecticut summer and many of them went there from time to time. Nobody knew exactly what happened that day, but Foone drowned. Perhaps his strength failed him or he struck his head while diving. Some said it was suicide.

It was August, 1841, nearly two years since the *Amistad* captives had been hustled ashore into captivity and another of their number was dead. The Africans were saddened and the determination to go home grew stronger and noisier, so that at last even the abolitionists had to listen to it.

All this time the people of Farmington were restless, too.

When the Africans arrived in their community, mothers clutched their children to them and reminded them that they must give a wide berth to the "cannibals." They would give money gladly if the abolitionists would take the Africans away.

Slowly, in the summer of 1841, a new fund-raising drive was begun. Lewis Tappan took the Africans to his own church, the Broadway Tabernacle, where they were exhibited at fifty cents a look. They went to the Colored Baptist Church in New York City, too, where they felt much more at home.

Much of the delay was occasioned by political and social considerations over which the Africans had no control. John Quincy Adams had suggested that the new administration of William Henry Harrison be approached to return the Africans to their native land at federal government expense, since United States naval officers had caused the trouble. But scarcely had the *Amistad* captives' court victory been celebrated and the Africans removed to Farmington than the President died, on April 4, 1841. The new President, John Tyler, must first get his feet on the ground and solve more pressing national problems than the affairs of three dozen Africans.

Ten days after President Harrison's death, another reason for the difficulty of the Africans in obtaining passage home became clear to Americans. The American Board of Commissioners for Foreign Missions had been approached to send the Africans back home and to establish a mission in Mendi. Some of the ardent abolitionists refused, however, to accept any proposition unless all the funds for the purpose were sequestered, and they were certain that no money from Southerners, other than abolitionists, would be used for the purpose.

"How would the people of Mendi receive a mission supported by the sale of Negroes in Virginia," *The Emancipator* asked editorially on April 15, "provided the whole story were told? The very idea of such a mission would make fiends laugh."

As the American Board of Missions would not allow the *Amistad* committee to dictate the conditions under which it would operate, the mission idea fell through at this stage. The abolitionists were very strong-minded about conditions under which the Africans would be allowed to go home. They could not accept the assistance of the American Colonization Society, which was sending regular shiploads of Africans back to their native soil, because this organization, too, was tainted with Southern funds.

So the Africans stayed on in Farmington, working the fields for their own support, devoting regular hours to the study of the Bible, and of English, to the learning of hymns and prayers, when they were not being exhibited to earn money for the cause.

The *Amistad* committee forged ahead in its loneliness. By September, however, signs of progress could be seen.[3] A plan was formulated to employ one surveyor and two Negroes, plus the interpreter James Covey, to go to Sierra Leone and then to Mendi country to determine whether a mission could be supported in the Mendi land. If it could be, then the captives would be sent home with the mission.

It was a good plan, but expensive, and so it languished as the abolitionists kept arguing among themselves. But later in the fall they began a search for white and Negro preachers who would be willing to go to the Mendi land and establish the mission. By October 21 the newspapers reported that the captives would be sent off "in a very few weeks" accompanied by white missionaries. One missionary had been found — the Reverend William Raymond.[4]

The appeal to the federal government for a ship, or transport aboard American warships, fell on relatively deaf ears. John Tyler was a Virginian. The slavery issue was becoming much too heated to be treated lightly. Indeed, as early as February of that year, even as the *Amistad* case was under consideration by the Supreme Court, the New York *Post* had published two full columns of incendiary material bearing on the case, but actually dealing with slavery in the South. "A marked fear is shown in certain quarters," said the *Post*, "lest by restoring to

liberty a set of men notoriously kidnaped and forcibly carried into bondage we may in some distant manner graze
the question of slavery in our country. The people in this part
of the country will not endure such a view of the question.
If the people of the South have their jealousies, so have the
people of the North."[5]

During the *Amistad* affair, and after it, slavery was rapidly
becoming a sectional issue, which it had not been earlier (for
example, when the *Amistad* captives were taken, slaves, although few, were still legally kept in Connecticut).

In November the abolitionists sent a number of the *Amistad*
captives on a broad fund-raising tour of New England. Singbe
and half a dozen of the others were sent to Boston, Salem,
Lowell, Worcester, Northampton, Springfield, and other cities
to take part in public meetings and show their progress. They
exhibited their skill at prayers, they read from the Bible, they
showed their handwriting and some specimens of words and
sentences.[6]

Although the Reverend and Mrs. William Raymond were
the only missionaries committed to the establishment of the
Mendi mission, the committee hoped to have still more, particularly missionary families. "It is exceedingly desirable," a
committee statement noted, "that a colored minister should also
go." Applicants were referred to Amos Townsend of New Haven,
John T. Norton of Farmington, S.S. Cowles of Hartford, and
Lewis Tappan in New York.

That month another two missionary couples were found — the
Reverend and Mrs. James Steele and Mr. and Mrs. Henry
Wilson, teachers, who were prepared to go to the African wil-
derness for a number of years. Time was growing short, for a
ship had been engaged, and it was hoped it would sail before
the wicked weather of December enveloped the Atlantic Ocean.

They would leave via the barque *Gentleman,* and travel to
Sierra Leone, the free port where there was no danger of an

incident. Thence they would be led into Mendi country by the
Amistad captives themselves, because several of the surviving
thirty-five men had visited Sierra Leone and knew the way.

All the whites were fiery abolitionists. Indeed, James Steele
and his wife came from that hotbed of abolition, Oberlin, Ohio,
where he had decided to become a minister after involvement
in an attempt to prevent the lynching of a Negro.

In mid-November the *Gentleman* was ready to sail for Africa.
Day after day boats pulled alongside the anchorage off Staten
Island bringing supplies for the mission, enough to last the
missionaries for a full year.

In Connecticut, on November 17, the *Amistad* captives were
taken to the First Church of Farmington for one last meeting,
and when it was over (having raised about $1,500 for the
cause), the Africans were taken to a boat on the canal that
ran between New Haven and Northampton, and headed south,
carrying parcels of the clothing, furnishings, and money they had
earned and received as gifts.

Soon they were in New York, where Lewis Tappan had
arranged a grand meeting at his Broadway Tabernacle. Reverend Pennington of the Hartford Negro church led the prayers.
A.F. Williams of the committee gave a history of the captives.
The captives gave a show. One read the 124th Psalm. One read
part of the fifth chapter of Matthew. They conducted a spel-
ling bee, to show their fluency in English. Ka-le, the little boy
who had written to John Quincy Adams, spelled out the words
"B-l-e-s-s-e-d a-r-e t-h-e p-u-r-e i-n h-e-a-r-t." They also sang a
hymn in English: "When I Can Read My Title Clear."

Kinna, eighteen years old, gave an account of his kidnaping
in Africa, told of the Lomboko slave *barracoon,* of the horrors
of the slave ship to Havana, of the fight on the *Amistad,* and
their siezure off Long Island. Then he answered questions.

"What will you say to your people in Africa when you reach
home?" asked one man.

"I will tell them what I have learned in the Bible — will tell them about God, about Jesus Christ coming into the world to die for sinners...."

As a revival the meeting was an unqualified success, and the show was concluded by a native song, which the Mendians sang in a far more animated manner than they had the hymns.

That night, Reverend S.S. Jocelyn of the *Amistad* Captives Committee publicly gave instructions to the missionaries who would accompany the Africans, abjuring them to keep the faith and teach the natives the joys of Christianity, and above all to stay out of business, which would destroy the faith of the natives in them.

Singbe, who had assumed the power and dignity of a chief, now arose and spoke to all in Mendi — his English not being equal to the occasion. Kinna interpreted. It was a long speech, in essence it was a speech of thanks to those who had befriended them, a promise to pray for them, thanks to those who sent the missionaries with them, and a promise to take care of the missionaries in the Mendi land.

The pastor of the Broadway Tabernacle gave a sermon on the need for missionary work among the Africans, and the multitude sang the African's favorite hymn, "From Greenland's Icy Mountains," which also happened to be a strongly abolitionist hymn, the favorite of many of those in attendance.

On the next night, November 22, the Africans performed before a largely Negro crowd at the Zion Methodist Church. The service was similar to that of the previous evening, except that a letter of good wishes from John Quincy Adams was read and the speakers were different, many of them Negro. Singbe repeated his speech, more or less, of the evening before. The evening ended in much the same way, except that since this was a Negro Church, at the end of the service the Negroes clustered around the Africans to shake their hands and wish them Godspeed on the way back to their home land.[7]

The farewell sessions continued in and around New York City

until Thursday, November 25. On Thursday morning the *Amistad* captives boarded the *Gentleman*. The next day a steamboat was engaged to tow the sailing ship down to the lower end of the harbor to quicken the passage and to give Lewis Tappan and his friends one last chance to speak to the Africans and say farewell.

All assembled in the cabin of the steamboat. The meeting began with a prayer and a hymn, and then Lewis Tappan spoke. He told Singbe to take care of the missionaries, and he adjured the missionaries to care for the souls of the Africans.

Singbe responded for the Africans.

By then the steamboat had reached the lower harbor and it was time for the *Gentleman* to be away. The Lord's Prayer was said, everybody embraced, and the *Amistad* captives and the missionaries sailed away, leaving a tearful crowd of abolitionists behind them.

The *Gentleman,* having missed the tide, anchored down harbor for the night, but at dawn was outward bound, on a fine Saturday morning, for the port of Sierra Leone.

17/Home to Africa

The *Gentleman* sailed east to Africa, stopping at the Cape Verde islands to replenish its water supply and take on fresh provisions. In the middle of January the ship arrived at Freetown, in Sierra Leone colony, and the passengers disembarked. They were home in Africa at last.

Almost immediately the civilization that the abolitionists had worked so hard to install into the *Amistad* captives was shown to be veneer, and it started peeling the first day ashore, when the old sights and old smells and old sounds reached them.

Mr. Raymond, the chief missionary, had attempted to make a triumphal entrance into Sierra Leone, scarcely realizing that freed slaves were nothing new in this colony. His march into the town was a dismal failure, with the Africans shedding civilization and Christianity at every step.

The British officials assigned the *Amistad* captives and their missionaries a house of their own. The idea was to have them all stay together and return to Mendi land, where the missionaries would establish a permanent mission and where Singbe would settle down as headman of the village or perhaps even king of the region. But within hours the Africans began de-

212

serting the group. Singbe became quarrelsome when advised that the supplies brought for the mission did not belong to the Africans but to the mission. Singbe also learned at Freetown that in the Mendi tribal wars, most of his family had been captured and sold into slavery.

It was a dismal beginning.

Mr. Raymond sent this sad word home to the mission backers and went on to establish his mission. He sent an advance party to Mendi land, accompanied by Singbe and a few of the other Africans, but the report was not encouraging. While Singbe was gone, all but ten of the Africans had lost faith and deserted. The missionaries settled down far from the Mendi land they had hoped to dominate and waited for word from home. In a short time Singbe, too, deserted them. Soon it was apparent that only the very young, the three little girls and those who had no particular memories of Africa, would be loyal to the mission.

After a time Singbe came back to the mission, without his Christian ways but, with a new African wife and a grasping hand. He quarreled with the missionaries and left them once more, to return to Mendi land, became a chief, and, ironically, a *slave trader*. But eventually he came back to the American missionaries when he did not prosper in Africa, and he remained as an interpreter at the Mendi mission station.[1]

Singbe died at the mission in 1879.

It could not be said that Reverend Raymond and the Mendi mission failed; they had simply underestimated the difficulties and overestimated the effects of two years of enforced training in civilized ways on the *Amistad* Africans. The mission was joined in 1846 with three other similar missionary committees and became the American Missionary Association, which eschewed relations with the evil slaveholders of the South.[2] It then continued successfully.

Slowly the Africans reverted to their old ways. Only one of the little girls, Margrov, grew up to become a practicing Christian.

She was to be the last survivor of the *Amistad* captives. She studied at American schools and became a teacher at the Mendi mission. She was living proof of the missionary's growing understanding that Christians are made early, not late.

In the spring of 1841, after the United States Supreme Court had freed the *Amistad* captives and given the naval officers their salvage rights, an outraged Spanish minister presented a formal demand for indemnity from the federal government.

Minister Argaiz asked for restitution of the losses suffered by the owners of the *Amistad* and its cargo and for an assurance that the case should "never serve as a precedent in analogous cases which may occur."

Daniel Webster was Secretary of State at this time. He received the message and immediately called on his old acquaintance John Quincy Adams for advice because Adams knew more about the Spanish treaty and the *Amistad* case than any other politician in Washington. Adams gave him a copy of Roger Sherman Baldwin's legal argument before the Supreme Court, which dealt in detail with the treaty and United States laws. He also gave Daniel Webster this advice: do not knuckle under to the Spaniards.

Webster waited three months before replying to the Spanish demands. In the interim he consulted with President Tyler. He said he could not see how the Spanish-American treaty had been violated, that the salvage payment was perfectly justified under

215

the circumstances, and that the Negroes of the *Amistad* were not legally slaves. He invited Señor Ruiz and Señor Montes to bring their cases for damages into the American courts, which were open to them. If the United States government had brought injury to anyone it would be glad to pay indemnification, he said, but in this case the government did not see any injury.[1]

The correspondence continued for nine months, without any change in Webster's mind. Minister Argaiz specifically demanded $47,405.62½, which included the value of the slaves. Argaiz also indicated to Webster that payments due the United States under other obligations would be withheld if the Spanish claim was not paid. Webster took offense, asserting that this was extortion, and immediately wrote Washington Irving, the American minister to Spain, to see if the Minister's statement was true. He wrote immediately, but the letter was three months in reaching Madrid. The Spanish government indicated there had been no such intent, so honor was satisfied — but by the time Webster learned this, the matter had taken a new course.[2]

All this activity had consumed the time until it was late in 1842. The *Amistad* captives were long back in Africa and widely scattered, free men, except perhaps those who were recaptured and re-enslaved in the continuing slave trade of the Spanish and Portuguese.

President Tyler was willing to made amends to the Spaniards for wrongs, real or fancied, that they might have suffered. The amount of money was not large, compared with other claims against governments, and the good-will of Spain seemed worth it. Tyler recommended that the amount of salvage allowed to the officers of the brig *Washington* be refunded to the Spaniards as proof of American good faith.[3]

In the early months of 1844 C.J. Ingersoll, chairman of the House of Representatives Committee on Foreign Affairs, introduced a bill that would give the Spaniards $70,000, an amount that would also compensate them for the loss of the men enslaved and then freed by the United States government. In this report it was very apparent that the *Amistad* affair was inextricably mingled with the internal politics of the United States, and that slavery, which until the 1830's had been more or less a subterranean issue, was rapidly becoming the single most divisive question on the American scene.

The House Foreign Affairs Committee asked that 10,000 copies of its report be printed and circulated widely among newspaper editors and persons of significance in the country, hoping to persuade, but instead the report brought about sharp debate, by extending the issue of the *Amistad* to consideration of internal problems.

The report was long and rambling, containing a complete, if slightly inaccurate, history of the *Amistad* case. But most members of the House committee proceeded further. They denounced the courts for having interposed themselves between the executive and his supposed function of carrying out the treaty with Spain. They attacked the judicial decisions handed down by the District Court, the Circuit Court, and the Supreme Court. Finally, the committee extended the argument to make it a defense of the institution of slavery in the United States.

The motion to print 10,000 copies poured fat into the fire, for it was an outright admission that the *Amistad* case would be used as propaganda for the cause of slavery. But the matter probably would have brought a sharp clash in any event because of the intemperance of the language of the report, as evidenced by the concluding paragraph: "When the Federal courts of justice err, Congress alone can rectify it. It is by act of Congress alone that this debt of national honor to Spain can be paid, as it ought to be, by signal proof to the world that none shall be wronged — not even by judicial authority — without redress, in the United States."[4]

In the *Congressional Globe* of that session of Congress, the index contained the following listing for the case: "Remarks on the subject of paying for the Negro pirates on the schooner *Amistad*," which gives some indication of the feelings that this case aroused even among members of Congress, and how small words defined large issues.[5]

When the proposal of printing 10,000 copies of the House committee's report was brought to the floor, the manner in which the advocates of slavery had twisted the *Amistad* case for their own use aroused the anxiety and anger of Northerners — and not only abolitionists. Representative Joshua R. Giddings of Ohio was the first to speak on the subject. Opposing the measure, he spoke for an hour in tones as bitter and denunciatory as those of the advocates on the other side. John Quincy Adams was prepared to speak next against the measure, but the Giddings speech carried the day. The motion was tabled.

Adams felt strongly that the bill represented a misuse of public funds. Indeed, he wrote in his diary that "seven years in a penitentiary cell would be a strictly just retribution for the report."[6] In 1845 Adams published the address he had planned to make before the House. It accused the advocates of slavery of espousing "false and spurious principles of international law," and attempting to disseminate a "putrid mass of slander" to the unsuspecting public.

The advocates of payment simply had gone too far. They had attacked the abolitionists: "A lawless combination, insisting that these blacks were guilty of no offense, resisted their being punished or tried in this country, or their extradition for trial and punishment in Cuba...."

They had attacked the press: "Zealots, with the help of the press, resisted the course of justices...."

They had attacked Great Britain: "But the fanatical denunciation of Negro slavery, which latterly passed over from England to America, created these blacks heroes and martyrs...."

They had attacked the respected and highly respectable Dr. Madden: "A salaried spy...."

They had defended the Spanish Inquisition as superior in justice to the United States government as it was constituted.

And so the Representatives from the North took the opposite position, insisting that the *Amistad* captives should be compensated for the loss of their ship, since they controlled it when it was seized, and that they should also be compensated for their stay in jail. (This would have brought up some interesting problems if it had carried because nearly all the *Amistad* Negroes had by then disappeared into the wilds of the African bush.)

In the acrimony much smoke was created and bitter words were spoken to add to the growing pile that would eventually feed the conflagration of civil war. The bill to compensate the Spaniards and settle the *Amistad* question failed, quite lost in the larger issue of American slavery.

Spanish Minister Argaiz had learned much from the uproar created when his correspondence with Secretary Forsyth was published. During the period that this matter was under consideration by the House of Representatives, he was very quiet, managing only to keep the issue open, trusting that recompense would be paid. In 1844 he was succeeded again by Don Añgel Calderon de Barca, who brought the matter to the attention of the new Secretary of State, John C. Calhoun. The issue was much too serious by this time to be handled casually, or even as a matter of simple compensation of damages between nations. Calhoun did little with it for the very good reason that it had reached him in December of an election year: A new President had been elected, and it would be up to him and his administration to handle the issue.

In the spring of 1845 the *Amistad* affair was brought to the attention of President Polk by his Secretary of State, James Buchanan. In the spring of 1846 Buchanan sent a note to Chairman Ingersoll of the House Foreign Affairs Committee, again suggesting that the Congress settle the matter by appropriating money to pay the Spanish claims. He was cautious about expressing an opinion, but put it in the light of its being and remaining an embarrassing issue between the two countries, "highly prejudicial, in many respects, to the interests of the United States."[7]

One might say that the Spanish were slow to learn the intricacies of American politics; or one might say that in the growing dispute over slavery, every aspect of American government that touched on this subject caused unceasing argument that left no room for the "normal" course of action. Either statement would be generally correct. From their point of view the Spaniards had been assured of the good offices of the United States district attorney who prosecuted the original *Amistad* cases, the Attorney General of the United States, the Secretary of State, even the President of the United States! More recently they had the good offices of several Presidents, Secretaries of State, and the chairman and majority of the House of Representatives Committee on Foreign Affairs — and still their demands got nowhere! Was it any wonder that the Spanish government and its ministers were confused and annoyed by the train of events in the United States relative to the *Amistad?*

It is a measure of the slavery issue in the United States in 1845 and 1846 that this remarkable situation could occur.

The result of Secretary Buchanan's correspondence with Chairman Ingersoll was a second committee report, very much like that of 1844. The report languished in the House of Representatives.

In the United States Senate, however, Southern sympathizers tacked a rider onto an appropriation for the payment of civil and diplomatic officials, calling for $50,000 to be divided among the various *Amistad* claimants. Secretary Buchanan wrote that he had studied the treaty and the case and felt that the Spanish claims were just under the treaty. President Polk concurred.

In the House of Representatives the steamroller faltered, for in its path stood frail John Quincy Adams. "Old Man Eloquent" he was called now, partly because of his spirited attack on the

Van Buren administration before the Supreme Court. Adams led the opposition to the payment of any money to the Spaniards, and the single speech he made on the floor of the House during that session was devoted to the subject of the *Amistad*. It had long been a *cause célèbre* with him, and he would not now see the cause dirtied and destroyed by payment of the Spanish claims.

Adams's opposition was based on several aspects of the affair: primarily he said that since there was not the shadow of legality to the Spaniards' claim, to pay such claims would be to rob the people of the United States and cast doubts upon the integrity of the United States Supreme Court. Further, to pay the claims would be to discard the decision of the high court, and if this was to be done, it must be done by a thorough rehearing of the whole business and not simply on the demands of the Secretary of State, who might believe the claim to be just or might simply wish to get out from under a trying situation (which was much more the case in Buchanan's position).

On March 2, 1847, the United States House of Representatives voted on the issue. Here came one of a new variety of votes that were to plague Congress unceasingly for the next fourteen years: a vote on a purely sectional basis, based on support of or opposition to slavery. John Quincy Adams might be going back beyond this issue to the questions of constitutionality and the responsibilities of the various branches of government to one another and to the people at large; his fellow Congressmen were not nearly so highly motivated. From the South came 40 votes in the House for the Senate amendment to the appropriations bill. From the North and West came 113 votes against it. The amendment was killed, and the *Amistad* case went into yet another phase, hanging like an albatross on the necks of the executive and legislative departments.[8]

The Spanish government took the issue up with the United States *chargé d'affaires* in Madrid, and again it was brought to

President Polk's attention. In December, 1847, he made it part of the subject of his annual message to Congress; again the issue was brought up in House and Senate, and the fate of the bills and amendments was the same: by sectional votes in the House and by non-sectional votes in the more responsible Senate.

Thwarted, facing another election in 1848, the Polk administration did not mention the *Amistad* affair again, and so it sat, waiting. John Quincy Adams died, stricken in the House that February, and the strongest advocate of the constitutional and moral principles involved in the *Amistad* affair was gone. From then on, the considerations were almost entirely on the basis of domestic American politics.

Zachary Taylor, slaveholder but constitutionalist and a defender of the Union, did not choose to bring up the *Amistad* affair with Congress in his brief administration, yet it continued to rankle, and the Spanish ministers in Washington never let it be forgotten. It was a thorn in the path of friendly Spanish-American relations — indeed, it had grown to be a whole thornbush.

In January, 1853, nearly twelve years after the final ruling of the case in the Supreme Court, President Millard Fillmore attempted to achieve a settlement of the claim and devoted a special Presidential message to the subject.

Nothing happened.

In his first annual message to Congress, President Franklin Pierce acknowledged the validity of a Spanish claim and recommended its rapid settlement.

Nothing happened.

After 1856, President James Buchanan seriously attempted to settle the affair, for he had been familiar with it as Secretary of State, and many bills were introduced. In February, 1858, a bill was introduced into the Senate accompanied by favorable report from the Committee on Foreign Relations. All such bills were blocked because of the growing feeling on slavery.

The *Amistad* affair became further complicated after 1844, when in a hurricane on the island of Cuba such damage was done that for a period afterward the provincial authorities had allowed foods and other goods to be imported without duty — and then suddenly the Spanish government collected back duties on all these goods. The Americans felt they had a claim against Spain in this case for more than $128,000, and efforts were made to collect it.

In negotiations over a period of time, the Americans at Madrid — Washington Irving and A.C. Dodge, in particular — were very much embarrassed because each time they tried to discuss the matter of the Cuba claims, the Spanish Foreign Ministry would bring up the matter of the *Amistad* claims.

The *Amistad* affair continued a sore spot in Spanish-American and North-South relationships, although it did not again come before the Congress directly.

An attempt was made to bind the two claims together (the Spanish paid part of the Cuba claims separately) in a complicated treaty that was drawn early in 1860 and submitted to the Senate on May 3. The treaty was defeated, almost entirely because of the *Amistad* affair's inclusion in the settlement, and the manner of its defeat was almost entirely political and sectional in nature. Twenty-four Democrats, one Republican, and one Southern Whig voted for the treaty, but twelve Republicans, one Democrat, two Northern Whigs, and two Free Soil members voted against it; thus it did not obtain the two-thirds majority necessary for consent. During nearly four administrations the executive branch had attempted to bring about some modus vivendi to better relationships with Spain, but Congress had, on principle, stood obdurate.

In 1861, when the American minister at Madrid, H.J. Perry, suggested that so much time had gone by that he could draw up a treaty for settlement of all outstanding claims without reference to any by name, Secretary of State Seward informed him that President Lincoln still would not honor the *Amistad* claim. He wrote:

> ... this government does not regard the so-called *Amistad* claim as having any valid obligation in law or conscience and can in no case consent to negotiate upon it. While, therefore, we shall not be critical as to the form of words to be used in describing the claims to be submitted to the proper joint commission, frankness requires that the exception of that supposed claim shall be expressed or at least distinctly understood.
>
> I am well aware that this instruction differs radically from admissions and acknowledgments made by several of the predecessors of the President. Each of them has considered the subject for himself, and pronounced upon it according to his own convictions. The new President, under the same obligation, instructs me to make known to you his disallowance of the claim in question. [Lincoln was familiar with the *Amistad* affair, for he had sat in Congress in 1847 and 1848 when the House was considering the matter.] It were indeed desired that there should be consistency in the action of the Government throughout successive administrations, especially when foreign nations are concerned, but justice and reason cannot be safely compromised by any government, even for the sake of preserving perfect consistency within itself through a series of years and in intercourse with foreign states.[9]

Another distinguished American was to become involved in the *Amistad* affair — Carl Schurz, successor to Minister Perry at Madrid. Schurz frankly explained to the Spanish Secretary of State, Saturnino Calderon Collantes, that for reasons of internal politics, the United States could not consider including the *Amistad* affair in any discussion of claims. He even suggested that Spain make an arbitrarily higher demand on some other claim, thus privately satisfying the *Amistad* claims without mentioning them.

To Secretary Seward's honor, when he heard of this plan he refused to accept the idea. The *Amistad* claim, he said, had no foundation "in justice or moral right," and the United States government could not deal with any such claims in any form at all.

The *Amistad* claims were finally dropped by Spain. Nearly a quarter of a century later, in responding to resolutions following an international conference at Milan to codify international law, Spain gave lip service to its own law that had so often been broken in Cuba. Spain's ancient laws, its government said in 1884, "have always recognized as free the slave who enters the territory [including its own] of a nation where slavery does not exist, or who seeks refuge on board a ship belonging to such a nation."[10]

That declaration was made nearly forty-five years after the beginning of the *Amistad* affair, and it put a final end to the question because if Spain wished, it could never retreat to renew demands on the United States.

Thus ended a footnote to history — the *Amistad* affair — in which the government of the United States, as badly divided among its branches as the nation was among sections, stood essentially for the highest concepts of liberty and justice. It was not a question of what the judiciary did, or the executive, or the legislative branch, but a question of the overall result of the interplay of the three branches on one another. And in this affair was shown the strength of the system of checks and balances, a system that could withstand the extreme influences and pressures exerted from every side. The Civil War did not break the system, and as the Northern legitimate government prosecuted the war, the principles that guided the determination of the *Amistad* affair remained.

The author is particularly indebted to librarians at the Yale University Library, the New Haven Colony Historical Society, and the Connecticut Historical Society in Hartford for the use of materials and a great deal of assistance. A particular debt is owed to Harry Harrison, chief of the circulation department of Yale's Sterling Library for the use of Yale's compilation of material relating to the *Amistad* captives.

Bibliography

ADAMS, CHARLES FRANCIS, (ed.). *Memoirs of John Quincy Adams.* Philadelphia: J.B. Lippincott, 1874.

The African Captives: Trial of the Prisoners of the Amistad *on the the Writ of Habeas Corpus before the Circuit Court of the United States for the District of Connecticut at Hartford, Judges Thompson and Judson, September Term, 1839.* New York: American Anti-Slavery Society, 1839.

Argument of John Quincy Adams Before the Supreme Court of the United States in the Case of the United States, Appelants, vs. Cinque and others, Africans, Captured in the Schooner Amistad *by Lieut. Gedney Delivered on the 24th February and the 1st March, 1814, with a Review of the Case of the* Antelope, New York, 1841.

Argument of Roger S. Baldwin of New Haven Before the Supreme Court of the United States in the Case of the United States, Appelants, vs. Cinque, and others, Africans of the Amistad. New York: S.W. Benedict, 1841.

BALDWIN SIMEON E. "The Captives of the *Amistad,*" *Papers of the New Haven Colony Historical Society,* Vol. IV.

BARBER, JOHN W. *A History of the* Amistad *Captives, being a Circumstantial Account of the Capture of the Spanish Schooner* Amistad, *by the Africans on Board; Their Voyage and Capture near Long Island, New York; with Biographical Sketches of Each of the Surviving Africans. Also an Account of the Trials Had on Their Case, before the District and Circuit Courts of the United States, for the District of Connecticut.* New Haven: E.L. and J.W. Barber, 1840.

BARTLETT, ELLEN STRONG. *The* Amistad *Captives: An Old Conflict Between Spain and America. (Bits of New England History,* Vol I.) New Haven: Yale University Library.

CALDWELL, ROBERT GRANVILLE. *Short History of the American People.* New York: Putnam, 1925.

COOPER, THOMAS and FENTON, HECTOR. *American Politics.* Philadelphia: Fireside, 1882.

FITZPATRICK, JOHN C. (ed.). *The Autobiography of Martin Van Buren. (Annual Report of the Amercian Historial Association for the Year 1819,* Vol. II.) Washington: Government Printing Office, 1920.

HOYT, EDWIN P. *John Quincy Adams*. Chicago: Reilly and Lee 1963.
——, *Martin Van Buren*. Chicago: Reilly and Lee, 1964.
McCENDON, R. EARL. "The *Amistad* Claims: Inconsistencies of Policy," *Political Science Quarterly*, September, 1933.
MARTIN, EVELINE (ed.). Nicholas *Owens Journal of a Slave Dealer*. London: Routledge, 1930.
MAYER, BRANTZ. *Captain Canot, or Twenty Years of an African Slaver*. New York: D. Appleton, 1866.
MORRIS, RICHARD B. (ed.). *Encyclopedia of American History*. (Rev. ed.) New York: Harper, 1965.
OWENS, WILLIAM A. *Slave Mutiny: The Revolt on the Schooner* Amistad. New York: John Day, 1953.
STERNE, EMMA GELDERS. *The Long Black Schooner: The Voyage of the* Amistad. New York: Aladdin, 1953.
26th Congress First Session, Document No. 185, House of Representatives, Executive, U.S. Department of State, Africans Taken in the Amistad, *Congressional Document Containing the Correspondence &c. in Relation to the Captured Africans*. (Reprint) New York: American Anti-Slavery Society, 1840.
WALTON, PERCY. *The Mysterious Case of the Long, Low, Black Schooner*. (*Documents and Memoranda*, Vol. VI.) Connecticut Historical Society, 1933.

Notes

Chapter One
1. *Encyclopaedia Britannica* (1958), XX, 781.
2. Richard B. Morris (ed.), *Encyclopedia of American History* (rev. ed; New York: Harper, 1965), p. 514.
3. Hartford *Courant*, September 17, 1839.
4. Thomas Cooper and Hector Fenton, *American Politics* (Philadelphia: Fireside, 1882).
5. Hartford *Courant*, September 17, 1839.
6. *Ibid.*
7. *Ibid.*
8. Brantz Mayer, *Captain Canot, or Twenty Years of an African Slaver* (New York: D. Appleton, 1866), p. 101.
9. Eveline Martin (ed.), *Nicholas Owen: Journal of a Slave Dealer* (London: Routledge, 1930), p.
10. Mayer, pp. 261-279.

Chapter Two
1. Mayer, p. 37.
2. *Ibid.*, p. 84.
3. John W. Barber, *A History of the Amistad Captives, being a Circumstantial Account of the Capture of the Spanish Schooner Amistad, by the Africans on Board; Their Voyage and Capture near Long Island, New York; with Biographical Sketches of Each of the Surviving Africans. Also an Account of the Trials Had on Their Case, before the District and Circuit Courts of the United States, for the District of Connecticut* (New Haven: E.L. and J.W. Barber, 1840).
4. *Executive Documents, 1st Session 28th Congress, December 1883*, IV, 17.
5. Hartford *Courant*, November 29, 1839.
6. *Ibid.*, September 10, 1839.
7. *Argument of Roger S. Baldwin of New Haven Before the Supreme Court of the United States in the Case of the United States, Appelants, vs. Cinque, and others, Africans of the Amistad* (New York: S.W. Benedict, 1841.)
8. Hartford *Courant*, November 29, 1839.

Chapter Three
1. New York *Sun*, August 31, 1839.
2. *Argument of Roger S. Baldwin....*
3. Hartford *Courant*, September 3, 1839.
4. Barber.

5. Hartford *Courant,* September 3, 1839.
6. *Ibid.,* August 27, 1839.
7. Ellen Strong Bartlett, *The Amistad Captives: An Old Conflict Between Spain and America. Bits of New England History,* Vol. I. (New Haven: Yale University Library).
8. Norfolk *Beacon,* August 24, 1839.
9. Hartford *Courant,* August 28, 1839.
10. Bartlett.
11. Bartlett.
12. Hartford *Courant,* August 28, 1839.

Chapter Four

Much of this chapter is derived from the Barber account and from the New York *Sun* account, which occupied several columns in the issue of August 31, 1831.
1. Bartlett.
2. *Ibid.*
3. Hartford *Courant,* September 3, 1839.
4. New York *Sun,* August 31, 1839.
5. Hartford *Courant,* September 3, 1839.

Crapter Five

1. Hartford *Courant,* October 2, 1839.
2. *Ibid.,* September 3, 1839.

Chapter Six

1. Harford *Courant,* September 3, 1839.
2. Edwin P. Hoyt, *John Quincy Adams* (Chicago: Reilly and Lee, 1963), pp. 136-139.
3. Barber, pp. 9-10.
4. Simeon E. Baldwin, "The Captives of the Amistad," *Papers of the New Haven Colony Historical Society,* IV, 336-337.
5. Hartford *Courant,* September 9, 1839.
6. *Ibid.*
7. *Ibid.,* September 6, 1839.
8. Baldwin, "The Captives of the Amistad," p. 338.
9. Hartford *Courant,* September 11, 1839.
10. *26th Congress First Session, Document No. 185, House of Representatives, Executive, U.S. Department of State, Africans Taken in the Amistad, Congressional Document Containing the Correspondence rc. in Relation to the Captured Africans,* (Reprint; New York: American Anti-Slavery Society, 1840).
11. *Ibid.*
12. *Ibid.,* pp. 5-6.
13. Hartford *Courant,* September 17, 1839.
14. *Ibid.*

Chapter Seven

1. John C. Fitzpatrick (ed.), *The Autobiography of Martin Van Buren. Annual Report of the American Historical Association for the Year 1918*, Vol. II. (Washington: Government Printing Office, 1920), pp. 131-132.
2. *The African Captives: Trial of the Prisoners of the Amistad on the Writ of Habeas Corpus before the Circuit Court of the United States for the District of Connecticut at Hartford, Judges Thompson and Judson, September Term, 1839* (New York: American Anti-Slavery Society, 1839), p. 8.
3. *Ibid.*, p. 9.
4. *Ibid.*, p. 10.
5. *Ibid.*
6. *Ibid.*, p. 13.
7. *Ibid.*, p. 14.
8. *Ibid.*, p. 15.
9. *Ibid.*, p. 16.
10. *Ibid.*, p. 18.
11. *Ibid.*, p. 21.

Chapter Eight

1. Hartford *Courant*, September 21, 1839.
2. *The African Captives*, p. 25.
3. *Ibid.*, p. 27.
4. Document No. 185, p. 25.
6. *Ibid.*
7. *The African Captives*, p. 30.
8. *Ibid.*, p. 37.
9. Document No. 185, p. 27.

Chapter Nine

1. Hartford *Courant*, September 19, 1839.
2. *Ibid.*, *Courant*, October 16, 1839.
3. Waterbury *Republican*, November 8, 1964.
5. *Ibid.*
6. Barber, p. 19.
7. *Ibid.*

Chapter Ten

1. Document No. 185, p. 42.
2. *Ibid.*, p. 38.
3. *Ibid.*, p. 41.
4. *Ibid.*, p. 10.
5. *Ibid.*, p. 12.

6. Confidential letter of Attorney General Grundy, Letter Book B, Attorney General's Office, January 15, 1834-October 1, 1850 (National Archives)

Chapter Eleven

1. Baldwin, "The Captives of the Amistad," p. 344.
2. Hartford *Courant*, November 20, 1839.
3. *Ibid.*
4. Hartford *Courant*, November 29, 1839; New York *Advertiser*, November 25, 1839.

Chapter Twelve

1. Document No. 185. p. 13.
2. Baldwin, "The Captives of the Amistad," p. 344.
3. Document No. 185, p. 14.
4. *Ibid.*, p. 16.
5. Baldwin, "The Captives of the Amistad," p. 344.
6. Document No. 185., p. 18.
7. *Ibid.*, p. 20.
8. *Ibid.*, p. 21.
9. Baldwin, "The Captives of the Amistad," p. 346.
10. Charles Francis Adams (ed.), *Memoirs of John Quincy Adams* (Philadelphia: J.B. Lippincott, 1874), X, 131.
11. Hartford *Courant*, December 30, 1839.
12. *Ibid.*
13. Twenty-one Pencil Sketches by Charles Allen Dinsmore, Yale University Library Gazette, January, 1935.
14. Bartlett, p. 72 ff.
13. Twenty-one Pencil Sketches by Charles Allen Dinsmore, Yale University Library Gazette, January, 1935.
14. Bartlett, p. 72 ff.
15. Buell G. Gallagher, "Amistad Incident," *The Talladegan*, May, 1941.
16. Document No. 185. p. 47.
17. Barber, pp. 20-22.

Chapter Thirteen

1. Hartford *Courant*, January 16, 1840.
2. *Ibid.*
3. *Ibid.*
4. *Ibid.*
5. *Ibid.*
6. *Ibid.*, January 15, 1840. (On January 15 and 16, the *Courant* ran a complete account of the trial and the judge's decision.)

Chapter Thirteen

1. Hartford *Courant*, February 10, 1840.
2. Document No. 185, p. 36.
3. *Ibid.*
4. Baldwin, "The Captives of the Amistad," p. 350.
5. *Ibid.*, p. 346.
6. Document No. 185, p. 2.
7. Hartford *Courant*, April 2, 1840.
8. *Ibid.*
9. Document No. 185, p. 2.
10. *Ibid.*, p. 30.
11. *Ibid.*, p. 42.
12. *Ibid.*, p. 34.
13. *Ibid.*, p. 36.
14. *Ibid.*, p. 48.
15. Bartlett, p. 360.
16. Percy Walton, *The Mysterious Case of the Long, Low, Black Schooner. Memoranda and Documents*, Vol. VI. (Connecticut Historical Society, 1933), p. 82.

Chapter Fifteen

1. Barber, p. 28.
2. Hartford *Courant*, August 28, 1840.
3. Hoyt, pp. 139-141.
4. Adams, *Memoirs of John Quincy Adams*, X, 393.
5. *Ibid.*, p. 396.
6. Baldwin, "The Captives of the Amistad," p. 352.
7. *The Emancipator*, New York, March 25, 1841.
8. Adams, *Memoirs of John Quincy Adams*, X, 399.
9. *Ibid.*, p. 429.
10. *Argument of Roger S. Baldwin . . .* , p. 30.
11. *Ibid.*, p. 32.
12. Adams, *Memoirs of John Quincy Adams*, X, 429.
13. *Argument of John Quincy Adams Before the Supreme Court of the United States in the Case of the United States, Appelants, vs. Cinque and others, Africans, Captured in the Schooner Amistad by Lieut. Gedney Delivered on the 24th February and the 1st March, 1841, with a Review of the Case of the Anteolpe, New York, 1841*, p. 9.
14. *Ibid.*, pp. 16-17.
15. *Ibid.*, p. 20.
16. *Ibid.*, p. 131.

17. Adams, *Memoirs of John Quincy Adams*, X, 431.
18. *Argument of John Quincy Adams . . .* , p. 54.
19. *Ibid.*, p. 134.
20. Baldwin, "The Captives of the Amistad," p. 00.
21. *Ibid.*, pp. 360-361.
Chapter Sixteen
1. Waterbury *Republican*, November 8, 1964; Hartford *Courant*, March 20, 1841.
2. *Farmington, Village of Beautiful Homes* (Connecticut Historical Society, privately printed): Richard M. Bissell, Jr., *Historical Sketch of Farmington*, (Connectitcut: Finley Bros.).
3. Hartford *Courant*, September 2, 1841.
4. *Ibid.*, October 21, 1841.
5. *Ibid.*, February 3, 1841.
6. *Ibid.*, November 1, 1841.
7. *Ibid.*, December 21, 1841.
Chapter Seventeen
1. Baldwin, "The Captives of the Amistad," p. 364; William A. Owens, *Slave Mutiny: The Revolt on the Schooner Amistad*, (New York: John Day, 1953).
2. *Ibid.*, pp. 364 ff.
Epilogue
1. Baldwin, "The Captives of the Amistad," pp. 364 ff.
2. R. Earl McClendon, "The Amistad Claims: Inconsistencies of Policy," *Political Science Quarterly*, September, 1933.
3. Baldwin, "The Captives of the Amistad," p. 366.
4. *27th Congress, 1st Session House Report*, p. 426.
5. Baldwin, "The Captives of the Amistad," p. 367.
6. Adams, *Memoirs of John Quincy Adams*, XII, 186.
7. McClendon, p. 400.
8. *Ibid.*, p. 401.
9. Perry Seward Correspondence, Department of State, National Archives.
10. Baldwin, "The Captives of the Amistad," pp. 369-370.